HARPER CHASE

Nefarious Crimes: Unsolved Murders Vol. 1

Contents

Introduction   1

Murder of Kristy Jones   3

Setagaya Family Murders   13

Murder of Wil Hendrick   30

Killing of Chandra Levy   39

2001 Anthrax Attacks   56

Killing of Geetha Angara   76

Murder of Sarah Pryor   90

Murder of Robert Wone   98

2006 Ulvila Homicide   113

Lane Bryant Shooting   123

Murder of Lindsay Buziak   137

Noida Double Murder   145

Murders of Dyke and Karen Rhoads   171

Introduction

In the shrouded corners of history, where whispers of unsolved murders linger like ghosts, a tapestry of untold stories and unexplained mysteries unravels. These cases, cloaked in shadows, reveal a truth more unnerving than fiction, not as conjurings of imagination but as unresolved enigmas left in the wake of real tragedies. They represent a foray into the heart of such mysteries, exploring cases that have puzzled detectives, haunted families, and captivated public imagination for years, sometimes centuries.

The allure of an unsolved murder lies not in the morbid details alone, but in the human stories intertwined with it. Each case bears unanswered questions: Who was responsible? What was their motive? In an era of advanced forensic science and technology, how do such crimes remain unsolved? The absence of answers creates a void that is both unsettling and irresistibly intriguing.

Unsolved murders are not confined to distant history or sensational serial killers. They occur in quiet neighborhoods, bustling cities, and places where such violence seems improbable. They happen to individuals who never envisioned their names in the dark annals of unsolved crimes.

Delving into these mysteries involves exploring psychological, sociological, and forensic aspects. Advancements in technology, like DNA profiling, have revitalized cold cases, offering hope where there was none. Yet, even with these tools, some mysteries remain out of reach, their secrets locked away by time, circumstance, or the elusive nature of human behavior.

This exploration is more than a recounting of facts and theories; it's a reflection on the human cost of these crimes. Behind every unsolved murder lies a story of a life cut short and a circle of family and friends grappling with a painful absence. The impact on communities is profound, where the shadow of an unsolved crime can linger for generations, casting doubt and fear.

Perhaps the most compelling aspect of unsolved murders is their reflection on society and human nature. These cases highlight the imperfections of the justice system, the limitations of investigative methods, and a collective fascination with the macabre. They prompt a confrontation with the uncomfortable reality that sometimes justice is elusive, and evil goes unpunished.

In these mysteries, stories of resilience and hope emerge. Dedicated law enforcement officers, persistent journalists, and determined family members refuse to let these cases be forgotten. Their perseverance is a testament to the human spirit's resilience in the face of the unknown.

These narratives are not merely chronicles of unsolved murders; they represent a search for truth in a world where answers are elusive. They remind of the ongoing quest for understanding, justice, and peace for the lost.

Prepare to traverse the shadows of history and the human heart. These stories are more than tales of murder and mystery; they are echoes of the eternal human quest to make sense of the senseless and find light in the darkest places. Welcome to the world of unsolved murders.

Murder of Kristy Jones

In the year 2000, Kirsty Jones, a 23-year-old Liverpool University graduate from Tredomen, Wales, embarked on a journey that was meant to be a thrilling chapter in her life. With a degree in hand and a spirit filled with wanderlust, she planned to explore the world for two years, seeking adventures far from her home, where her parents, Glyn and Sue Jones, managed a sprawling 400-acre beef and sheep farm. Described by her mother as "bright, intelligent, independent," Kirsty was seen as someone with the entire world at her feet, a young woman on the cusp of discovering life's myriad possibilities.

Her journey, rich with the promise of new experiences, led her across diverse landscapes and cultures. After visiting places like Malaysia and Singapore, Kirsty found herself drawn to the enchanting city of Chiang Mai in Thailand. This destination, famed for its serene Buddhist temples, a vibrant tapestry of nightlife, and a historic walled center, has long been a magnet for backpackers, digital nomads, and expatriates. They are drawn not only to its cultural richness but also to the affordability of living there. Websites like ALittleAdrift.com and Numbeo.com highlight the city's appeal with estimates of living costs ranging from $600 to $1800 per month, a stark contrast to places like Seattle where rent is significantly higher.

In her quest for authentic experiences, Kirsty, like many travelers her age, opted for the humble yet vibrant life of hostels. These establishments offer not only an economical stay but also a chance to meet fellow travelers from all corners of the globe. It was with this spirit of adventure and exploration that Kirsty arrived in Chiang Mai on August 4, 2000. She checked into the Aree Guesthouse and Massage School located on Moon Muang Road Soi 9. The accommodation, modest yet sufficient, cost her just 60 Thai baht (THB) per night, approximately $1.73, providing a simple space with just enough room for a bed and her dreams.

The Aree Guesthouse, where Kirsty Jones checked in during her travels in Chiang Mai, carried a reputation tinged with controversy. Known among the backpacker circles as a place where drugs were easily accessible, it had a shadowy past. In 1999, the establishment faced a severe crackdown when the Royal Thai Police shuttered its doors for six months following the tragic demise of a backpacker due to a heroin overdose. Whether Kirsty was aware of Aree's infamous history with drugs remains a matter shrouded in mystery.

Despite the guesthouse's dubious reputation, Kirsty's adventure in Thailand seemed to unfold with joy and discovery. She immersed herself in the local culture and nature, capturing the majestic beauty of elephants and the lush jungle during a three-day trek in the hills with a tour group. Her journey also led to new friendships, notably with fellow British backpackers Nathan Foley, aged 27, and Sarah Wiggett. This trio, united by their shared love for exploration, spent their days meandering through Chiang Mai's unique spots, from a quaint Thai bakery to a lively Irish bar, creating memories in the city's eclectic mix of locales.

The evening of August 9, 2000, marked another memorable day for the group as they enjoyed the flavors of a local Thai restaurant. However, the night took different turns for each of them. Foley departed early to make a phone call to his girlfriend in Spain, leaving Kirsty and Wiggett to explore the bustling Chiang Mai Night Bazaar. This vibrant market, a hub for artisans, street food, and souvenirs, was alive with the energy of night-time commerce. Wiggett returned to her accommodation at 11:30 p.m., but the details of Kirsty's return to Aree, a 25-minute walk from the bazaar, remained uncertain, including whether she made the journey back alone.

The following day, on August 10, 2000, a grim discovery was made. Kirsty's lifeless body was found in her room at the Aree Guesthouse, 15 hours after she had been brutally raped and strangled. The scene was harrowing: she lay face down, partially clothed, with a piece of dark blue sarong, which she had been wearing as a skirt, wrapped tightly around her neck.

The initial delay in reporting her body and the subsequent handling of the investigation cast a dark shadow over the case. The crime scene was compromised almost immediately, with reporters and a Thai television crew gaining access to Kirsty's room before the police could properly secure it. This chaos at the crime scene was emblematic of the disarray that plagued the investigation from its onset.

In a bid to gather firsthand information, British journalist Andrew Drummond, stationed 400 miles south in Bangkok, reached out to local reporter Pim Kemasingki. Drummond's intention was to have Kemasingki visit the crime scene and relay the details back to him, hoping to piece together the tragic and mysterious circumstances surrounding Kirsty's untimely death.

Pim Kemasingki, a reporter intimately familiar with the workings of the Thai media landscape, shed light on a crucial aspect of crime reporting in Thailand. She explained that local reporters often arrive at crime scenes before law enforcement officials, thanks to their access to police radios. This practice, while instrumental in gathering news quickly, had a detrimental impact on Kirsty Jones's case. Kemasingki estimated that at least 20 individuals had entered Kirsty's room before it was properly secured by the Royal Thai Police (RTP). In a chaotic breach of protocol, these intruders inadvertently tampered with potential evidence, touching Kirsty's belongings and bed sheets, thereby contaminating any clues the perpetrator might have left.

The BBC, recognizing the complexity and international relevance of the case, enlisted Kemasingki as their interpreter the following day. She worked alongside British reporter David Willis, navigating the intricacies of the investigation and the cultural landscape of Thailand to provide comprehensive coverage.

The murder of Kirsty Jones quickly escalated into an international news story, captivating audiences worldwide. The RTP, under intense scrutiny, identified seven individuals as potential suspects. This diverse group comprised five foreigners and two Thai nationals, each with their own complex background and potential motives.

Among the suspects was Australian Stuart Crichton, aged 28, who was also a guest at the Aree Guesthouse. The RTP arrested him after discovering heroin and marijuana in his room, although it was unclear how this linked him to the murder.

Another intriguing figure in the case was Glen, an ex-Mormon with a mysterious past. He claimed to have worked as a CIA spy and was in Thailand to recover from head injuries sustained in a car accident. His presence added another layer of complexity to the already convoluted investigation.

Stephen Trigg, a 27-year-old known heroin addict, had been traveling for four years before his arrival in Chiang Mai. On the night of August 10, 2000, he reportedly heard Kirsty's desperate screams for help, pleading, "Leave me alone, leave me alone, get off me, get off me." Despite the alarming nature of these cries, Trigg, along with other guests who had emerged to investigate, retreated to their rooms, mistakenly assuming the incident was a domestic dispute. Trigg and another suspect considered intervening but ultimately decided against it. Trigg later expressed his belief that the assailant was likely a Westerner, basing this on the nature of Kirsty's screams.

Nathan Foley, another key figure, had spent the earlier part of the evening with Kirsty and Wiggett. He did not return to the Aree Guesthouse until

3 a.m. on August 11, 2000. The RTP subjected him to an intense 13-hour interrogation. Foley, an Australian traveling to Kent, England, to visit relatives for the first time, as reported by The Guardian, found himself entangled in a complex web of suspicion and inquiry.

Andy Gill, a 32-year-old expatriate from Northern Ireland, found himself at the center of the investigation surrounding the tragic murder of Kirsty Jones. Gill, the owner of the Aree Guesthouse, was a figure surrounded by varied narratives. Some accounts suggested that he had acquired the guesthouse using funds from an inheritance, while other reports hinted that he had sold a property in Andorra to finance this venture in Thailand.

Gill's lifestyle in Chiang Mai was an interesting blend of leisure and fitness. He was an active member of the Chiang Mai Hash House Harriers, a unique running club that catered to expatriates who balanced their love for drinking with a desire to stay fit. This group's activities painted a picture of a vibrant expat community in Thailand, with Gill as one of its more colorful characters.

At the time of Kirsty's murder, Gill claimed to have an alibi, insisting he was not at the guesthouse. He mentioned that a Thai friend could vouch for his absence, claiming he returned to his room only after the crime had occurred. Gill, who had been living in Thailand for 12 years, had integrated into the local community, even having a Thai girlfriend.

However, Gill's situation became complicated post-murder. He chose to voluntarily disappear, driven by the fear that authorities would discover his visa had expired two years prior. This act of evasion cast a shadow of suspicion over him. His eventual arrest at a local bar on August 12, 2000, was initially for the expired visa, resulting in a fine of 2,000 Thai Baht (approximately $57.49). However, the Royal Thai Police later escalated the charges, accusing him of conspiracy to commit murder, a charge Gill vehemently denied.

Surin Chanpranet, variably referred to in reports as Channet and Janpamet, aged 47, emerged as another pivotal figure in this intricate case. As the manager of Aree and the head of a Thai massage school on the premises, Chanpranet was deeply entwined with the day-to-day operations of the guesthouse. Intriguingly, according to The Daily Telegraph, the property was registered in Chanpranet's name, a common practice in Thailand where foreigners are restricted from owning land. The discovery of amphetamines, marijuana, and a postcard depicting a nude foreign woman in bondage in his room further intensified the suspicion around him.

Chanpranet found himself under arrest in connection with Kirsty's death. He was with Stephen Trigg on the night of the murder, and both had advised other guests to disregard Kirsty's screams, attributing them to a domestic dispute. Despite this suspicious behavior, Chanpranet produced an alibi, albeit a questionable one, provided by his wife, Panthipa. Suffering from a brain injury and mental instability, Panthipa claimed her husband was with her in their room throughout the night, except for the brief moment when he and Trigg responded to the noise from Kirsty's room.

Approximately five weeks after the murder, Chanpranet made a shocking claim. He alleged that he had witnessed Gill engaging in sexual activity with Kirsty through the curtains of her room. However, he later altered his statement, saying he had only seen Gill leaving her room. Chanpranet's death in 2007 brought a close to his chapter in this complex and unresolved case, leaving many questions unanswered.

Narong 'Abraham' Pojanathamrongpongse, a 34-year-old tour guide from Chiang Mai, became a dramatic figure in the investigation following Kirsty Jones's murder. In a startling turn of events, Narong disrupted a police press conference with a harrowing tale. He claimed that he had been abducted by a group of men, whom he believed were undercover police officers. According to his account, these men subjected him to a terrifying ordeal involving kidnapping, drugging, stripping, and torture.

Pim Kemasingki, documenting the unfolding drama, reported Narong's disturbing allegations. He was allegedly threatened with execution and coerced to confess to Kirsty's murder, with his attackers demeaning his hill tribe heritage and pressuring him to "help the country" by taking the blame. Narong, however, stood firm and refused to confess. After losing consciousness during this ordeal, he later awoke in a jail cell at the police station. Kemasingki, having observed visible signs of abuse on Narong, found his story of kidnapping and torture credible.

Complicating the narrative further, there were conflicting reports about a Thai tour guide named Johnny, who reportedly led Kirsty and a group of nine backpackers on a three-day hiking expedition near Chiang Mai. Some sources speculated that this guide was Narong himself, one of the last people to have seen Kirsty alive.

Another key figure in this tangled web of stories was Nong Nee, a 17-year-old maid at the Aree Guesthouse. Initially, Nee told the Royal Thai Police that she discovered Kirsty's body between 4 p.m. and 4:30 p.m. on August 10, 2000. However, she later recanted this statement, admitting that she had lied. Instead, she claimed that Chanpranet had found Kirsty's body much earlier, between 10:30 a.m. and 2 p.m., well before the murder was reported to the police. Some accounts even suggested that it was Gill who discovered the body.

Nee's testimony further revealed that both Chanpranet and Gill had instructed her to remain silent while they "figured things out." Gill was apprehensive about the police uncovering his expired visa, while Chanpranet was concerned about the drugs in his room.

As the investigation proceeded, Thai police were convinced that the perpetrator was among the seven men they had identified. They expressed optimism about making an arrest soon after the murder. However, the investigation was marred by a series of missteps and controversies, starting with the compromised crime scene and escalating with a series of sensational claims and counterclaims.

Before the release of the autopsy results, Colonel Prasit Thamdi, the Chief of Police for the Municipality, made a premature and controversial statement. He suggested that Kirsty had engaged in consensual sex with her killer, who then accidentally strangled her during the act. This statement, which implied a personal relationship between Kirsty and her assailant, was widely reported in over twenty newspapers globally. However, the autopsy results painted a different picture, revealing that Kirsty had been violently sexually assaulted. In response to the backlash from his statement, Thamdi was quickly reassigned to Isan, a region in northeast Thailand.

In this complex and convoluted case, DNA evidence emerged as the crucial element that could potentially prove guilt or innocence. Yet, even this critical piece of evidence would become entangled in the bizarre and troubled narrative of the investigation into Kirsty Jones's murder.

The investigation into Kirsty Jones's murder was marked by an intensive search for DNA evidence, which became a focal point in the quest for justice. Seminal fluid recovered from inside Kirsty's body and on the sarong used to strangle her was sent for DNA testing. In a collaborative effort, all eight suspects, along with Chanpranet's friends, comprising three Thais and a Frenchman, voluntarily provided blood samples for testing.

Amidst the scientific endeavor to find the killer, Colonel Suthep Dejraksa shared with Pim Kemasingki a bizarre and unsettling rumor. On the night of Jones's murder, there was talk of a foreign man who allegedly paid several tuk-tuk drivers for their seminal fluid, speculating that this foreign individual might have planted the sample inside Kirsty's body to mislead the investigation.

In a further twist in 2002, Thai police revealed that transvestites Jessada

Wiriyasakul, aged 28, and Cha Kesarachai, aged 26, confessed that Chanpranet had employed them to source false DNA to plant at the crime scene, ostensibly to protect the real killer.

Dr. Tanin Bhoopat, a respected figure in forensic medicine at Chiang Mai University, provided crucial insights into the case. He confirmed that the violent sexual assault Kirsty suffered had caused the seminal fluid to lodge deep inside her body, occurring before her death. Moreover, Dr. Bhoopat identified the DNA as belonging to an Asian male.

Despite these efforts, DNA testing ultimately cleared all 11 male suspects, including the foreign nationals who were then permitted to leave Thailand. The murder charge against Gill was dropped in November 2000, leading to further scrutiny of the Royal Thai Police's handling of the case.

In response to concerns voiced by the Jones family, Dyfed-Powys Police from Wales traveled to Thailand in 2001 to assist in the investigation. They were joined by Welsh forensic experts who secured the killer's DNA, with results revealed in January 2002. Dyfed-Powys Police determined that while the DNA did not match Narong's, it showed a remarkable similarity to his DNA, leading them to believe it belonged to one of Narong's relatives.

This revelation prompted the media to intensely search for members of Narong's family who might match the DNA profile, but their efforts were in vain.

In 2011, the investigation took another turn when Welsh police pursued a tip from a YouTube video uploaded by an Australian. The video suggested that a Thai professor at Chiang Mai University and a Thai tourist police officer, both seen near the Aree guesthouse around the time of Jones's murder, should be investigated. Although a DNA test ruled out the police officer, the professor initially refused to provide a sample. He eventually relented, and his test results were negative.

After two decades of twists and turns, the case reached a somber conclusion. In August 2020, the Thai police officially closed the Jones murder case as the 20-year statute of limitations on murder had expired. This meant that even if the killer were to be identified in the future, they could never be charged for the crime, leaving a permanent shadow over this tragic and unresolved case.

Setagaya Family Murders

In the vibrant heart of Japan, as the world ushered in a new millennium, the Miyazawa family embodied the essence of a traditional Japanese household, yet with their own unique story. Unlike America's Y2K frenzy, Japan celebrated the dawn of 2001 with a serene embrace of the future.

Mikio Miyazawa, a 44-year-old father, was a cornerstone of Interbrand, a global marketing giant known for coining "Wi-Fi" and shaping the identities of Microsoft and Nissan. Though his specific role remains a mystery, his congenial nature made him a beloved figure at the company, a man without enemies.

Yasuko Miyazawa, the compassionate 41-year-old mother and wife, dedicated her life to teaching and nurturing her two children, Niina and Rei. Her warmth and kindness radiated throughout their home and community.

Niina, a spirited second-grader, reveled in the joys of soccer and ballet, embodying the playful innocence of childhood. Meanwhile, young Rei faced his own challenges, grappling with a speech impairment that worried the family, prompting them to seek professional help.

Their home in Setagaya, a burgeoning development chosen in 1990, was more than just a residence; it was a sanctuary for growth and happiness. Setagaya, the second largest of Tokyo's twenty-three districts, offers a tranquil contrast to the bustling city, with its residential charm and proximity to Tokyo Bay.

As the world celebrated a new century, the Miyazawas, like many in Japan, looked forward to the promise of new beginnings, their lives a tapestry of modernity and tradition.

The Miyazawa residence was a unique architectural blend that resembled a duplex. Externally, it presented as a single house, but internally, it was divided into two separate living spaces. This design ingeniously housed the Miyazawas alongside Yasuko's relatives: her mother, sister, and brother-in-law, fostering a close-knit family environment.

Seven family members cohabited in this bifurcated home, yet, intriguingly, there was no internal passage linking the two halves. To traverse between them required stepping outside and using separate entrances.

A significant aspect of their home was its proximity to a local park. This park, a longstanding fixture, was undergoing expansion by the city. This development led to a mass exodus of neighbors, leaving the once bustling community with barely a trace of its former vibrancy. Only the Miyazawas, their relatives, and two other families remained, creating an almost ghostly atmosphere in the neighborhood.

The skate park, located just behind their home and separated only by a fence, was the epicenter of activity in the otherwise quiet expanse. This brought its own set of challenges for the Miyazawas. Mikio had recently confronted some noisy teenagers there, and there were reports of him dealing with members of the Bosozoku, a youth motorcycle gang.

With the park's expansion plans escalating the foot traffic behind their home, the Miyazawas were contemplating a move. By December 2000, they had decided to relocate to a new home in a few months, hoping to endure the disturbances from the skate park just a bit longer.

Tragically, fate had other plans, and the family would never get the opportunity to make that move.

In the days leading up to the New Year, the Miyazawa family's neighborhood was steeped in a series of peculiar incidents that went beyond Mikio's confrontations with local troublemakers.

The summer had brought disturbing signs of animal cruelty in the area. There were unsettling reports of rodents found harmed and stray cats tortured, with one disturbing account of a cat found without its tail. These troubling rumors, though impeded by language barriers, added a sinister undertone to the community's atmosphere.

On Christmas Day, Yasuko observed a mysterious car repeatedly parking in front of their home, an odd choice given the availability of more convenient parking spots. This unusual activity was out of place in the usually tranquil neighborhood.

Then, on December 27th, an individual believed to be in his forties was seen lingering around the Miyazawa residence. Though the proximity to the park made the presence of strangers not uncommon, in hindsight, this observation seemed ominous.

By December 29th, just before the turn of the century, another strange sighting occurred at Seijogakuenmae Station, a short distance from the Miyazawas. A man dressed in skater attire, noticeably underdressed for the weather and carrying a backpack, drew attention.

Significantly, on this same day, a man fitting this description was believed to have purchased a sashimi knife at a nearby supermarket. The uniqueness of this purchase made it notable for later investigation.

The following day, December 30th, a man matching this earlier description was spotted near Sengawa Station, closer to the Miyazawa home. This person, estimated to be between thirty-five and forty years old, seemed to be gradually converging on the Miyazawa residence in Setagaya.

On the evening of December 30th, a seemingly ordinary day in the life of the Miyazawa family unfolded, unaware it would be their last. The air was filled with the anticipation of the upcoming New Year celebrations, a time that symbolizes new beginnings.

That evening, around 6 PM, the family is believed to have left for some last-minute holiday shopping. Although it's not clear if all family members were together, a sighting at a local shopping area around that time, coupled with a neighbor's observation of their missing car, suggests they were out as a family.

Yasuko, later in the evening, made a phone call to her mother, who lived in the adjoining unit. Such calls were a routine part of their daily lives, reflecting their close yet neighborly relationship. This particular conversation, likely about everyday matters, possibly included a simple invitation for her mother to join them or watch Niina.

Niina's visit next door to watch TV until about 9:30 PM pointed to a normal family evening. Nothing seemed amiss or out of the ordinary for the Miyazawas at this point.

The final glimpse into their lives came from an email accessed by Mikio at approximately 10:38 PM. This work-related email required a password, indicating Mikio was the one who opened it.

This email check-in was the last confirmed activity in the Miyazawa household, a stark contrast to the horror that was soon to envelop their peaceful home.

As the clock neared ten on that fateful evening, an eerie disturbance rippled through the calm of Setagaya. A witness, strolling along the park path behind the Miyazawa house, caught the faint strains of what seemed like an argument emanating from within the walls of the family home. The sounds weren't alarmingly loud or filled with terrifying screams, but rather like a typical domestic spat, intense yet contained.

Around ninety minutes later, a different kind of sound pierced the night. A relative of Yasuko, residing in the adjoining unit, heard a startling bang from the Miyazawa's side. The exact time was unclear, but a television program schedule later helped pinpoint this unsettling moment.

Simultaneously, an individual was seen hastily moving along the path adjacent to the Miyazawa residence. This fleeting glimpse was one of the few indicators that something was terribly wrong that night.

The horror that unfolded inside the Miyazawa home remained hidden from the world for several more hours.

Meanwhile, nearby, a taxi driver was embarking on a late-night fare that would later haunt his memory. He picked up three middle-aged men, whose silence during the ride struck him as unusual. The hour was late, and their destination was a nearby station, an odd choice for such a time.

One of the passengers, he later recalled, had a wound. A bloodstain left on the cab's backseat was a disturbing but not immediately alarming detail. The driver, understandably, found this peculiar and unsettling, a memory that would remain vivid in his mind.

It wasn't until the next day, when the grim events of that night in Setagaya began to unravel, that the significance of these seemingly unrelated occurrences would come into horrifying focus.

On the morning of New Year's Eve, a day that should have been filled with joyous anticipation, Yasuko's mother experienced a chilling silence that would forever alter her life. She attempted to call her daughter's family to discuss plans for the afternoon, but was met with an eerie silence; the call didn't even connect.

Unbeknownst to her, a sinister act had severed the phone lines to the Miyazawa home. With a sense of unease, she ventured outside and made her way to the house that held so many cherished memories of her daughter, son-in-law, and beloved grandchildren.

Upon arrival, her repeated doorbell rings were met with no response. Following her instincts, she used her keys to enter, stepping into a deafening stillness. The absence of any sound was the first ominous sign that something was terribly amiss.

The harrowing truth began to unfold as she discovered Mikio's lifeless body at the foot of the staircase. The sight of the 44-year-old father, who had succumbed to multiple stab wounds, was a horrific introduction to the tragedy that had struck her family.

Ascending the stairs, her worst fears were confirmed. At the top, she found Yasuko and her granddaughter Niina, both victims of a brutal and senseless attack. The extent of their injuries was staggering, a gruesome scene that indicated an overwhelming level of violence.

In a heart-wrenching moment, she reached out to touch her daughter and granddaughter, perhaps driven by a mixture of sorrow and a faint glimmer of hope. But the cold, lifeless bodies of Yasuko, with whom she had shared over four decades of life, and Niina, the granddaughter she had spent the previous evening with, marked a devastating reality.

The final blow came as she entered a nearby bedroom. There lay six-year-old Rei, the youngest of the family, who had been struggling with a speech impediment. He was found in his bed, strangled, leading investigators to believe he was the first to be attacked.

In a state of shock and despair, Yasuko's mother called the police. But the images of that day, the loss of her entire family in such a violent manner, were indelible scars that time could never heal.

The Tokyo Police, responding to the grisly scene at the Miyazawa residence, were as appalled and shaken as Yasuko's mother. They were acutely aware that this brutal annihilation of a family would send ripples of fear and horror throughout the community. The idea of an entire family being mercilessly slain in the quiet of the night by an unknown perpetrator was a chilling and deeply unsettling reality.

At the crime scene, the police set to work, meticulously combing through every detail to reconstruct the events of that tragic night. Yasuko's mother, sister, and brother-in-law, who lived next door, were interviewed for any unusual or suspicious occurrences they might have noticed.

The only notable anomaly they recalled was a loud thud heard around 11:30 PM. The timing of this noise was cross-referenced with a television program schedule, suggesting a possible timeline for the events. The police theorized that this thud might have been the moment when Mikio confronted the attacker. Given the nature of his injuries, they speculated he struggled with the assailant before being overpowered and thrown down the stairs.

Mikio's wounds, predominantly stab injuries to the neck, were consistent with a sashimi knife, which was later found in the kitchen. This particular knife, purchased just a day earlier from a local supermarket, was brought to the scene by the murderer. However, during the attack, the knife somehow broke, although the specific details of how this occurred are unclear. Based on evidence at the scene, the police surmised that the assailant used a second weapon, likely a knife from the family's own kitchen, to commit the rest of the killings.

A peculiar observation about Mikio's body was that he was still dressed in his business attire, suggesting he was attacked unexpectedly. There was an unverified report that he was wearing only one shoe, but this detail remains unconfirmed and should be considered with caution. The scene painted a picture of a sudden, unexpected attack, leaving little time for the family to react or defend themselves.

The tragic discovery of Yasuko and Niina's bodies requires a brief explanation of the Miyazawa family's home layout. The house had a unique architectural design, with a ladder at the top of the stairs leading to a second-story loft. This loft, equipped with a bed and television, was presumably where Yasuko and Niina were at the time of the attack, possibly watching TV or resting.

Both Yasuko and Niina were found at the bottom of the ladder that led to this loft. The brutality of their injuries was stark; they had been stabbed multiple times, with the extent of the wounds suggesting an attack that continued well after their deaths. This excessive violence led investigators to speculate about the killer's possible deep-seated aggression towards women and girls, a theory that, while distressingly common in such crimes, became a focal point in the subsequent investigation.

Rei, the family's young son, was found in his bed, having been strangled. Initially, the police were puzzled as to why Rei was spared the violent stabbing that claimed the lives of his other family members. However, as they delved deeper into the case, they concluded that Rei was likely the first victim. His final moments, spared from witnessing the horrific attack on his family, were nonetheless filled with a confusion and fear that a child of his age could scarcely understand. The quiet, unassuming nature of his death starkly contrasted with the chaos and violence that engulfed the rest of the Miyazawa household.

On the afternoon following the discovery of the Miyazawa family tragedy, a man in his thirties arrived at a medical center near Tobu Nikko Station, several hours north of Setagaya, the Tokyo district where the Miyazawa family resided. With numerous train connections between the two locations, the journey was not out of the ordinary.

This individual sought treatment for a severe hand wound, deep enough to expose bone. Despite the gravity of his injury, he was remarkably indifferent, raising the staff's suspicions. He wore a black down jacket and jeans, and chose not to disclose his identity or the circumstances behind his injury. After receiving treatment, he left the facility, which at the time was unaware of the horrific events that had unfolded in Setagaya.

Back at the crime scene, investigators found an abundance of evidence. Crucially, they quickly located the murder weapons: the sashimi knife purchased on December 29th and another kitchen knife from the Miyazawa's home, both found in the kitchen and stained with blood. The discovery of these weapons was a significant breakthrough, as many investigations struggle without such crucial evidence.

The Miyazawa home turned out to be a veritable goldmine of clues. The family's first aid kit had been opened, likely by Yasuko and Niina during the attack, as indicated by the blood-stained bandages found with Niina.

More disturbingly, the upstairs bathroom held a shocking piece of evidence: unflushed feces left by the killer. This oversight, whether due to ignorance of DNA testing or brazen confidence, provided a unique clue. Analysis of the waste revealed remnants of a sesame spinach dish with string beans, suggesting a meal consumed elsewhere.

In the years following the investigation, online sleuths have speculated on the nature of this meal, often described as mundane or typical of a home-cooked dish. This detail has led to the theory that the killer might have been living with his mother, a hypothesis that, while speculative, reflects the effort to understand the mind and circumstances of the perpetrator.

Scattered throughout the house were the telltale footprints of the assumed perpetrator, stamped in blood and dirt. These imprints, distinctively belonging to Slazenger shoes, sparked a wave of intrigue. While Slazenger shoes were common in Japan, the specific size of these footprints was peculiarly Korean, igniting theories about the assailant's origins.

Amid the chaos, detectives stumbled upon an unsettling discovery: bandages from the first aid kit, hastily used by eight-year-old Niina, along with towels and women's sanitary products, all smeared with unidentified blood. This grisly scene suggested a desperate struggle between Mikio and the attacker, hinting at an injury sustained by the assailant.

The urgency to test the blood samples was palpable, yet the painstaking process offered no swift answers. The police were left to comb through the maze of clues the killer had seemingly left behind, perhaps intentionally.

Among the most startling revelations were the various personal items abandoned by the killer. These included a gray "Crusher" hat, a black AirTech jacket, a distinctive white-and-purple long-sleeved shirt, black Edwin gloves, an untagged, multi-colored scarf, and a black handkerchief. These items, reminiscent of a skater's attire, seemed to have been discarded without a second thought.

The white shirt with purple sleeves, stained with blood, stood out. It was a style foreign to the family and was available only at Marufuru shops - the same retailer that sold the gloves and hat found at the scene.

Equally intriguing was the black handkerchief, meticulously ironed - an unusual practice for such an item, especially for a young skater. This peculiar detail led to speculations about the killer's living situation, possibly with a maternal figure. Additionally, traces of the male cologne Drakkar Noir found on the handkerchief.

The discovery of the clothing items at the crime scene revealed a curious detail: they had all been washed in hard water, rich in minerals and vitamins not commonly found in Japan's predominantly soft water system. This contrast in water quality hinted at the possibility that the killer might have a Korean background, as Korea predominantly uses a hard water system, aligning with the condition of the clothes.

In addition to the clothing, the perpetrator left behind a unique personal item—a "hip-bag." This peculiar accessory, a hybrid of a messenger bag, a small backpack, and a fanny pack, contained critical clues. Inside, investigators found skateboard grip-tape, traces of the Drakkar Noir cologne also found on the handkerchief, and, most intriguingly, sand.

Forensic science has made remarkable advances in the analysis of sand. Experts can now trace its origins to a specific region within a radius of approximately fifty to a hundred miles. The sand from the hip-bag pointed to an unexpected location: the Southwestern United States, near Edwards Air Force Base, roughly a hundred miles north of Los Angeles. This revelation suggested a potential military connection, raising theories about the killer being an airman stationed in Tokyo or an international contractor.

Some theorized that the meticulously ironed handkerchief indicated military discipline, aligning with this new military link. Despite these intriguing leads, the investigation was far from over. With no solid suspect in sight, detectives continued to unravel the complex web of evidence, hoping for a breakthrough in this perplexing case.

As time passed, the days blending into weeks and then into months, the police turned to the public for help, hoping someone might recognize the clothing left by the killer at the Miyazawa residence. Despite their efforts to trace the origins of these common items, sold by the thousands in Japan, the task proved daunting and ultimately unproductive.

Around a hundred days after the tragic incident, a small but potentially significant discovery was made not far from the Miyazawa home: a Buddhist statue depicting Jizo, a deity revered for protecting children in the afterlife. According to Eastern Asian Buddhist beliefs, Jizo safeguards the souls of children who pass away before their parents, shielding them from harm as they journey to the spirit realm.

Initially considered a piece of evidence, the police speculated whether the killer had left the statue as a symbol of guilt or remorse. Found along a creek bed in Setagaya, close to where the family lived, the statue stood as a poignant symbol of the lost lives and the unsolved crime.

Meanwhile, the police pieced together a probable sequence of events for that fateful night, leveraging their developing forensic technology. They concluded that the intruder likely entered through the second-story bathroom window, an entry that required significant physical ability. This window, situated at the back of the house and above a fence adjacent to a park, seemed the most plausible point of entry.

The investigation suggested a chilling scenario: the assailant first targeted six-year-old Rei in his bedroom, silently strangling the child in his sleep. The sequence of events thereafter became less certain. It was hypothesized that Mikio, working downstairs, was alerted by a noise and confronted the intruder on the stairs. This confrontation led to a struggle, resulting in Mikio's death at the bottom of the stairs, where his body was later discovered. The precise movements and actions of the killer within the house remained a subject of speculation and investigation, with detectives piecing together the grim timeline.

According to the evolving theory of the crime, the next tragic sequence involved Yasuko and Niina. The killer may have confronted them either in the third-floor loft or near the ladder leading to it. Evidence suggested that Niina, in a desperate attempt to tend to her injuries, used the first aid kit. It's theorized that the killer initially attacked them with a broken sashimi knife, then retreated to the kitchen for a replacement weapon, possibly leading Yasuko and Niina to believe, albeit briefly, that the danger had passed. They might have seized this moment to administer first aid, mistakenly thinking the assailant had fled.

Alternatively, it's conceivable that after Rei's murder, Niina and Yasuko encountered the intruder, leading to a struggle that drew Mikio upstairs. In this scenario, Mikio could have rushed to their aid, inadvertently leaving Rei, already a victim, behind. The ensuing altercation with Mikio may have ended fatally at the staircase, where the killer also broke his weapon and sustained an injury.

Needing a new weapon, the killer likely ventured into the kitchen, then returned to gruesomely conclude his assault on Yasuko and Niina. They might have been trying to escape to the loft, using the ladder as a potential barrier.

However, the investigation revealed a chilling postscript: the killer didn't immediately flee the crime scene. Instead, he lingered in the Miyazawa home for hours, a highly unusual behavior for a perpetrator. He neglected to cover the bodies of the slain family and eerily made himself at home, even resting on the living room sofa.

In a chilling display of detachment, the Miyazawa family's killer indulged in ice cream from their refrigerator, leaving behind wrappers bearing his fingerprints. These prints, found throughout the house, matched none of the family members.

The intruder also accessed the family's computer, located in the downstairs study. At 1:18 AM on December 31st, only hours after the family's likely time of death, the perpetrator browsed a theater website previously bookmarked by Mikio, who had a passion for theater. This peculiar activity raised questions: was this a twisted act by the killer, or had the murders occurred later than initially thought?

The computer was used again around 10:05 AM, this time to browse websites related to Mikio's company, Interbrand, and Yasuko's school. Intriguingly, the killer limited his browsing to sites the family had bookmarked, as if savoring the personal nature of his invasion. After about ten minutes, the computer was disconnected.

Throughout the night, the killer collected various ID and credit cards from the family, later found sorted near the sofa where he had slept. This behavior suggested an attempt to decipher PIN codes, but the cards were left behind, possibly to avoid further risk.

In a bizarre and unexplained act, the killer gathered an assortment of items—garbage, including ice cream wrappers, advertising leaflets, some of Mikio's work receipts, Yasuko's school documents, and feminine sanitary products with the killer's blood—and placed them in the bathtub. The motive for this remains unclear; it might have been an aborted effort to conceal evidence.

Before leaving, the killer is suspected of stealing around 150,000 yen from the family, equating to over a thousand dollars in American currency. However, more money was found in the study, suggesting that robbery was not the primary motive.

The notion of robbery as a motive was questioned. Notably, the family's valuables remained untouched, with only an old jacket belonging to Mikio missing. This detail added to the mystery surrounding the killer's intentions.

Complicating the investigation further, Yasuko's mother, who discovered the gruesome scene, initially recalled the front door being locked. This led investigators to speculate that the killer might have exited the same way he entered: through the second-story bathroom window. However, over time, her certainty about the door's status waned, leaving the exact exit method of the killer unclear.

In the years following the crime, now nearly sixteen since the incident, various pieces of evidence have been circulated and debated by internet sleuths. Unfortunately, some of this information has proven to be inaccurate or misinterpreted.

One such example involves postcards reportedly missing from the Miyazawa home. Early claims suggested that holiday greeting cards from friends and family had been stolen by the killer. However, this turned out to be a misconception. The postcards had been collected by an investigator as part of routine inquiries with the senders, a common practice in criminal investigations. Thus, the narrative of the missing postcards was debunked, revealing them to have always been in police custody.

Another piece of evidence that has been discredited is the presence of trace amounts of red dye at the crime scene. This finding led to speculative theories about the killer's involvement in methamphetamine production, with the red dye linked to chemicals used in the drug's manufacture. However, further investigation revealed that the dye was a common component in red highlighters, rendering these theories baseless.

These corrections are important to note, as they've been widely discussed on internet forums and have often been presented as crucial clues. Regrettably, much of the English-language coverage of this case is outdated, leaving a gap in accurate and current information for those following the case.

As the years passed, the mystery of the Miyazawa family murders remained unsolved, transforming the unidentified assailant into an almost mythical figure, akin to the urban legends of elusive criminals in Western lore. Despite the passage of time, in 2006, advancements in forensic science offered a new window into identifying the killer.

Forensic experts utilized DNA genome testing on blood samples found at the crime scene, revealing surprising details about the killer's ancestry. The analysis indicated that the perpetrator was likely of mixed race, not solely of Japanese descent. According to police sources cited by 'Japan Today', the killer's genetic makeup suggested a paternal lineage with East Asian roots—shared among Japanese, Chinese, and Koreans—and a maternal lineage traced back to the southern Mediterranean, possibly the Adriatic region.

This revelation opened up new possibilities regarding the killer's identity. While there remained a chance that he was a Japanese citizen, the lack of matching fingerprints over the years suggested otherwise. Especially in the post-9/11 era, with heightened global security measures and fingerprinting at borders, the likelihood of such an individual evading detection seemed slim.

The DNA evidence painted a picture of a killer with a complex ethnic background: potentially half East Asian and half Southern European. The paternal DNA markers were more common in Koreans but were also present in Chinese and Japanese populations, adding to the ambiguity of his exact ethnic origin.

In addition to the DNA findings, physical evidence left at the crime scene provided further clues about the killer's characteristics. His height was estimated to be around 175 centimeters (approximately five feet seven inches), deduced from the size of the clothing he left behind. The shoe size, specific to Korean measurements, was about 27.5 cm (just under eleven inches). The blood type of the assailant, determined to be type A, did not match any of the Miyazawa family members.

Despite the detailed profile of the killer, justice has remained elusive for sixteen years following the Miyazawa family murders. One of the significant ambiguities in the case is the number of perpetrators involved. Initially, the narrative has been framed around a single killer, but over time, alternative theories suggesting multiple assailants have surfaced, adding complexity to the investigation.

One factor fueling these theories was an incident involving a taxi driver who reported picking up three suspicious individuals on the night of the murders. Early reports highlighted a bloodstain left by one of these passengers, sparking speculation about its connection to the crime scene. However, subsequent developments or confirmations regarding this lead have been notably absent, suggesting it may have either been a dead end or an unrelated coincidence.

The multi-killer theory might have inadvertently sidetracked the investigation in its early stages. Rumors linked this theory with an alleged confrontation Mikio Miyazawa had with local skateboarders and bikers. Given that the killer's attire resembled that of a skateboarder, there was speculation that this might have been a deliberate ploy to misdirect or align with the known dispute. This angle was pursued, though it's unclear how significantly it impacted the overall investigation.

Additionally, some early journalistic reports raised the possibility that the killer or killers may have left the Miyazawa residence at some point during the night, possibly returning later. This idea could align with the multiple assailants theory, suggesting that while one intruder entered through the second-story window, others may have been let in subsequently.

However, it's important to emphasize that these remain theories, lacking solid evidence to firmly establish the involvement of multiple killers in the crime. The investigation, over the years, has not produced conclusive proof to support the idea that more than one person conspired or participated in the tragic events at the Miyazawa family home.

Murder of Wil Hendrick

In the early hours of a chilly January morning in 1999, the peaceful town of Moscow, Idaho was shaken by the mysterious disappearance of William "Wil" Hendrick, a vibrant 25-year-old college senior from the University of Idaho's theater department. Wil, known for his charismatic personality and his burgeoning career in acting, had recently achieved a significant milestone by securing a small role in a Hollywood action film, marking a promising turn in his journey as an aspiring actor.

That fateful night, after attending a lively party, Wil mysteriously vanished. His absence sent ripples of concern through his network of friends, fellow students, and especially his long-term partner, Jerry Schutz. Wil and Jerry, who had been in a committed relationship for five years, were well-regarded in the community, and Wil's disappearance left Jerry and others in a state of deep distress.

In a perplexing twist, Wil's car was discovered abandoned in downtown Moscow the day following his disappearance, adding to the growing alarm and unanswered questions. Despite extensive searches and widespread appeals for information, the case took a grim turn when, two years later, hunters stumbled upon Wil's remains in a secluded wooded area. The discovery transformed the missing person's case into a homicide investigation, a shocking development that reverberated through the University of Idaho and beyond.

The unsolved nature of Wil's case has haunted both the local community and those who knew him personally. The absence of clear motives or suspects has only deepened the mystery surrounding his untimely demise. Wil's life, so full of potential and promise, was tragically cut short, leaving behind a legacy of unanswered questions and a quest for justice that continues to this day.

On the evening of January 9, 1999, the usually quiet life of Wil Hendrick and his partner Jerry Schutz was disrupted by a pulsating energy that heralded the return of students from Christmas break to the University of Idaho. The couple was busy remodeling their kitchen, immersed in the task of creating a cozy, welcoming space in their home. However, the allure of reconnecting with friends at a party was too strong for Wil, a lively and sociable individual. Despite Jerry's decision to stay back and catch some rest, the two shared a heartfelt exchange of "I love you" before Wil departed, a moment poignantly etched in memory given the events that would unfold.

The party, hosted by Wil's friend Katie Payne, was a vibrant affair, buzzing with the excitement of students eager to share stories of their holiday adventures. Two separate gatherings were in full swing at Katie's residence. The third-floor revelers were mostly ex-athletes from the local high school, while the second-floor gathering in Apartment C was a lively mix of theater students, a group where Wil naturally blended in with his engaging personality and passion for the arts.

Amid the festivities, a concerning situation arose involving another of Wil's friends, Karen, who was dealing with some distressing issues with her boyfriend, who was part of the third-floor crowd. Wil, ever the protector of his friends, was deeply concerned. Kathy Sprague, another friend, was worried that Wil's protective nature, especially when fueled by alcohol, might lead to a confrontation.

The night was marred by tension, as police later reported that Wil was involved in several heated arguments with some attendees. This detail would later become a significant piece in the puzzle of Wil's mysterious disappearance.

The party began to wind down in the early hours, and around 2:30 a.m., Karen left for home. Katie, ensuring the safety of her friends, called Karen to check if she had reached home safely. But it was then that Katie realized Wil was missing. A quick check revealed that his car, which had been parked outside earlier, was still there, a detail that would soon change and add to the mystery.

By the morning of January 10, with Wil still not back home, a worried Jerry reached out to Katie around 11:30 a.m. The unsettling news that Wil hadn't stayed at the party all night and was nowhere to be found sent a wave of concern through Jerry. He promptly called other theater students who were at the party, but none had seen Wil since the party. The absence of any sightings or clues as to where Wil might have gone escalated the situation from a simple case of staying out late to something far more worrying.

On the chilly morning of January 10th, Jerry Schutz found himself walking through the doors of the Moscow Police Department with a heavy heart, gripped by a growing sense of dread. He was there to report his partner, Wil Hendrick, missing. Jerry's mind raced with worrying scenarios: perhaps Wil had inadvertently passed out in a secluded spot, maybe in a field, or worse, had tumbled into a ditch in a state of inebriation. The uncertainty was agonizing.

The disappearance of Wil set off a fervent search throughout Moscow. Jerry, joined by a group of friends and aided by the police, scoured the town for any sign of Wil or his car. Their efforts soon led them to a crucial discovery - Wil's 1984 brown, 4-door Pontiac, uncharacteristically abandoned near the intersection of Fourth and Jackson Streets, close to Friendship Square in downtown Moscow.

The car, unlocked and forlorn, held inside it a poignant clue - Wil's portfolio. This portfolio was a treasured compilation of all his artwork and costume designs, a testament to his creative spirit and aspirations in theater. Jerry knew instantly that something was amiss; Wil would never voluntarily leave such a precious item behind. Another alarming detail was the presence of Wil's work keys on the dashboard. Wil was meticulous about his keys, always keeping them either on his person or at home. Their unusual placement in the car indicated a disruption in Wil's usual habits, a red flag that something untoward had occurred.

Adding to the mystery was a can of Squirt soda found inside the vehicle. Wil's friends were adamant this wasn't his – he was known to always have two cups in the front of his car, one for cigarette butts and the other for chew spit, but never a third for a drink. This uncharacteristic presence of the soda can raised further questions.

The police conducted a forensic examination of the car, hoping to uncover evidence of foul play, but their efforts were in vain. There was no blood found, and all the hair samples matched Wil. The car, seemingly untouched by violence, offered no conclusive leads to his whereabouts. When the car was returned to Jerry, he noticed mud caked on the inside of the wheel wells, suggesting the car had been driven through unusual terrain. Additionally, the driver's seat was pushed back further than Wil's driving position, hinting at someone taller having driven the vehicle.

The investigation intensified as police interviewed students from the party with whom Wil had argued and conducted polygraph tests. All passed, deepening the mystery. Witnesses reported seeing Wil's car parked outside the party and later heard a car speeding away, gravel crunching under its tires in haste.

As reported by the _Lewiston Tribune_, the subsequent years were inundated with hundreds of tips and reported sightings of Wil across the nation, stretching from Florida to Las Vegas. The case attracted national attention, partly due to its timing – Wil, an openly gay man, had vanished just a year after the tragic murder of Matthew Shepard in Wyoming, a case that had spotlighted hate crimes against the LGBTQ+ community. This parallel drew the eyes of the media, casting a spotlight on Wil's case, yet despite the extensive coverage and numerous leads, the whereabouts of Wil Hendrick remained a mystery that continued to perplex and haunt all who knew him.

On a fateful day in September 2002, the tranquility of the Idaho wilderness was disrupted by a grim discovery. Four hunters, navigating through a remote area, stumbled upon a chilling scene: a partially exposed human skull and jaw bone, stark reminders of a life once lived. The remains, upon examination, were identified as those of Wil Hendrick, who had vanished mysteriously three years earlier. The inability to determine the cause of death, combined with the circumstances of the discovery, led investigators to suspect foul play, thus transforming the missing person's case into a homicide investigation.

This pivotal moment galvanized law enforcement agencies. The Moscow Police Department, Idaho State Police, Latah County Sheriff's Office, Lewiston Police Department, and the FBI collaborated to establish the Wil Hendrick Homicide Investigation Task Force. This multi-agency effort underscored the seriousness of the case and the determination to uncover the truth behind Wil's untimely demise.

In a telling 2002 press release, the Moscow Police Department disclosed the involvement of the FBI's Behavioral Analysis Unit from Quantico. The insights from these seasoned behavioral analysts brought a new dimension to the investigation. They posited that Wil's killer was likely not a stranger, and robbery was probably not the motive. This suggested a chilling possibility: Wil was likely acquainted with his killer, someone familiar with the Moscow-Pullman area, and the location where his body was eventually discovered. The analysts theorized that the perpetrator had not intended for Wil's remains to be found, adding a layer of premeditation and cold calculation to the crime.

Furthermore, the Behavioral Analysis Unit speculated that the offender might have left the area soon after the homicide, ostensibly for legitimate reasons, but driven by ties to the area and a morbid curiosity about the investigation, they likely returned. This profile painted a picture of a killer ingrained in the community, someone who might have been hiding in plain sight.

Fast forward to 2014, and the investigation was still active, with a renewed focus on the physical evidence. Advances in forensic technology presented a glimmer of hope. Investigators were in the process of re-examining the evidence, considering resubmission to the state crime lab for analysis using these newer methods.

Investigators explored various leads, one of which pointed towards an intriguing character who lived right beneath Katie Payne's apartment, where Wil had last been seen partying. This man, residing in the 1st floor apartment, recounted to the police a peculiar incident on the night of Wil's disappearance. He claimed that a drunken Wil had stumbled into his apartment, seemingly in a belligerent state and looking for a confrontation. However, according to the man, he managed to defuse the situation by simply turning Wil around and sending him back out. The police, diligent in their investigation, searched his apartment thoroughly but found no trace of any criminal activity. This lack of evidence led them to eventually rule out the man as a suspect in the case.

Another lead that piqued the interest of investigators emerged from an incident that occurred two months before Wil's disappearance. Jerry, Wil's partner, had fired a van driver who worked for his shuttle service. The termination was not amicable; Jerry recalled the man reacting with anger and resorting to using an anti-gay slur. Subsequently, this individual found employment with a long-haul trucking company in Lewiston, ID, approximately 30 miles south of Moscow.

In a curious coincidence, on the morning of Wil's disappearance, around 4:30 a.m., this former employee checked out a refrigerated truck from his new employer's dispatch. This detail, coupled with his known animosity towards Wil and Jerry, cast a shadow of suspicion over him. However, his complete lack of cooperation with the police investigation only deepened the mystery.

Adding to the intrigue, Rausch received a tip from a woman acquainted with the truck driver. She informed the authorities that the driver had expressed a sudden urge to retrieve his belongings from his trailer and mentioned plans to move to Florida. This move was particularly suspicious given that the driver lived in the same trailer park as Wil and Jerry. Wil, known for his sociable nature, had occasionally stayed at the man's home, especially on nights when he wanted to avoid arguments with Jerry.

Rausch described the driver's actions as "highly suspicious activity." Despite this suspicion, the lack of concrete information hindered the authorities from compelling the driver to undergo an official interrogation. This limitation left Rausch and his team in a state of frustration, as they felt hamstrung in their efforts to delve deeper into this potential lead.

Eventually, authorities managed to track down the man in Florida. Yet, even with this breakthrough, the driver remained uncooperative, continuing to evade the grasp of the investigation. A search of his trailer yielded no evidence of any crime, leaving the police with no viable option but to cease pursuing the driver as a suspect.

In 2014, a news article shed light on the intricate and often frustrating journey of the investigation into Wil Hendrick's disappearance. At the heart of this narrative was Wayne Rausch, who, at the time of Wil's disappearance, served as a detective in the sheriff's office. His initial involvement in the case was short-lived, as then-sheriff Jeff Crouch removed him from the case. Rausch recounted how he was barred from accessing even his own reports, with the case file being pass-coded to restrict his involvement. This period, marked by a lack of transparency and collaboration, led to a prolonged phase where Rausch, even after moving to patrol and before his eventual promotion to sheriff in 2004, remained largely in the dark about the progress of the case.

Upon assuming the role of sheriff, Rausch revisited the case, only to be met with dismay at the apparent lack of follow-up and progress. This stagnation was not just a professional frustration but also a personal one, given the emotional weight the case carried.

Keith Hendrick, Wil's father and a veteran law enforcement officer of 38 years, bore the anguish of his son's unsolved case until his passing in 2013. Despite his long career in law enforcement, the personal tragedy of losing his son to an unresolved crime brought not only heartache but also a sense of helplessness and unresolved questions that lingered for 14 years.

Keith, in an interview in 2008, poignantly expressed the deep hurt that overshadowed any thoughts of vengeance. His fear that the perpetrator might remain at large and possibly harm others was a haunting concern, rooted in his professional understanding of criminal behavior.

Wil's mother, Leslie, harbored the belief that her son was targeted because of his sexual orientation, a theory that resonated in the backdrop of Moscow's reputation as a gay-friendly community. The gay community, actively involved in the search efforts, was left shaken and filled with fear following Wil's disappearance. Kathy Sprague, a member of this community, in 2008, articulated the mix of disbelief, fear, and rampant speculation that enveloped them in the wake of the incident.

The quest for answers in Wil Hendrick's case continued, gaining national attention when 'Unsolved Mysteries' aired a segment on it in 2001, bringing the story to a wider audience.

Meanwhile, Jerry Schutz, Wil's partner at the time of his disappearance, has journeyed through the ensuing years, now in his 50s and working as a nurse. He continues to reside in Moscow, a city woven into the fabric of this enduring mystery. His life, forever altered by the events of that fateful day, stands as a testament to the enduring impact of unresolved tragedies and the relentless pursuit of closure and justice.

Killing of Chandra Levy

handra Levy, born into the warm embrace of family life in Cleveland, Ohio, was the cherished daughter of Robert and Susan Levy. Her early years were marked by a move across the country to Modesto, California, where she attended the esteemed Grace M. Davis High School. As a young woman deeply rooted in her cultural heritage, Chandra's family was an active part of Congregation Beth Shalom, a Conservative Jewish synagogue, which undoubtedly played a significant role in her upbringing and values.

Levy's academic journey took her to San Francisco State University, where she pursued her passion for storytelling and truth, earning a degree in journalism. Her career path began to take shape through significant internships and work experiences. She first honed her skills at the California Bureau of Secondary Education and later in the bustling political environment of Los Angeles Mayor Richard Riordan's office. These experiences were mere stepping stones to her ultimate academic goal – a master's degree in public administration from the prestigious University of Southern California.

In pursuit of practical experience to complement her academic endeavors, Levy ventured to the nation's capital, Washington, D.C. Here, she embarked on a challenging yet rewarding journey as a paid intern with the Federal Bureau of Prisons. Starting in October 2000, Levy joined the bureau's headquarters, where her responsibilities lay in the public affairs division. Her supervisor, Dan Dunne, bureau spokesperson, quickly recognized Levy's exceptional talent, particularly her adept handling of media inquiries. This was most notable during the high-profile case of Timothy McVeigh, convicted of the Oklahoma City Federal Building bombing. Levy's professionalism and competence in managing such a sensitive and complex matter were commendable.

However, Levy's journey took an unexpected turn in April 2001. Her internship, which had been a period of significant professional growth and learning, was abruptly terminated. The reason was a technicality - her academic eligibility had expired in December 2000. Despite this setback, Levy had already fulfilled the requirements for her master's degree and was preparing for a triumphant return to California in May 2001 for her graduation ceremony.

The mysterious disappearance of Chandra Levy began unfolding on May 1, 2001. This day marked the last confirmed sighting of Levy, setting in motion a perplexing and high-profile investigation. It wasn't until five days later, on May 6, that the Metropolitan Police Department in Washington, D.C., was alerted to her absence. Levy's concerned parents, calling from their home in Modesto, California, expressed their growing anxiety over not having heard from their daughter. In response, the police swiftly initiated a search, calling hospitals and visiting Levy's Dupont Circle apartment. The initial examination of her living space revealed no obvious signs of struggle or foul play, deepening the mystery.

The plot thickened on May 7, when Levy's father disclosed to the police a startling revelation: his daughter had been involved in an affair with a U.S. congressman. The following day, he named U.S. Representative Gary Condit as the alleged figure in the affair, a claim that Levy's aunt corroborated, having been confided in by Chandra herself. This development added a sensational twist to the case and propelled it into the national spotlight.

On May 10, armed with a warrant, investigators conducted a thorough search of Levy's apartment. They discovered her belongings - credit cards, identification, and mobile phone - neatly tucked away in her purse. Her suitcases, half-packed, suggested a trip either planned or abruptly abandoned. Her answering machine was full, echoing with the voices of worried relatives and two messages from Congressman Condit.

The investigation took a technological turn when police attempted to access Levy's laptop. In a critical misstep, a police sergeant, lacking the necessary technical expertise, accidentally corrupted the internet search history. It took computer experts a month to painstakingly reconstruct this data, revealing Levy's online activities on the morning of her disappearance. She had browsed websites related to Amtrak, Baskin-Robbins, Condit, Southwest Airlines, and even checked a weather report from The Washington Post. Her final search, at 12:59 p.m., was for Alsace-Lorraine, a region in France. Intriguingly, at 11:33 a.m., Levy had searched for information about Rock Creek Park in The Washington Post's "Entertainment Guide," and a minute later, clicked a link for a map of the park. This clue led detectives to theorize that Levy might have planned to meet someone at the Pierce-Klingle Mansion, the park headquarters.

The search for Levy intensified in the lush expanse of Rock Creek Park. On July 25, 2001, a determined team of three D.C. police sergeants and 28 cadets scoured the Glover Road area but came up empty-handed. Even a subsequent search yielded no clues.

Amidst the growing despair, Levy's parents and friends were relentless in their efforts to keep her story alive in the public eye. They organized numerous vigils and press conferences, united in their poignant plea to "bring Chandra home."

The enigma surrounding Chandra Levy's disappearance quickly escalated into a national controversy, capturing the undivided attention of the American news media. At the heart of this unfolding drama was U.S. Representative Gary Condit, whose connection to Levy sparked a whirlwind of speculation and scrutiny. Condit, representing the congressional district where Levy's family resided, was a married man. Initially, he staunchly denied any romantic involvement with Levy. Despite the police not labeling him as a suspect, Levy's family expressed their suspicions about Condit's evasiveness, suspecting he might be withholding crucial information about Levy's whereabouts.

The plot thickened in early July 2001. Unnamed police sources revealed that Condit had, in a dramatic turn of events, confessed to an affair with Levy during a confidential interview with law enforcement on July 7. Condit's depiction of Levy to the police painted her as a health-conscious vegetarian, abstaining from alcohol and smoking. He had believed that Levy intended to return to Washington, D.C., after her graduation and was reportedly taken aback upon learning that her apartment lease had concluded.

The investigation into Levy's disappearance then directly intersected with Condit's personal life. On July 10, detectives executed a search of Condit's apartment. Another layer was added to the complex narrative when flight attendant Anne Marie Smith stepped into the limelight. She claimed that Condit had advised her against cooperating with the Federal Bureau of Investigation regarding his personal affairs. This interaction prompted federal authorities to probe Condit for potential obstruction of justice, especially since Smith, too, was entangled in an affair with him, yet had no acquaintance with Levy.

Condit's response to the escalating situation was marked by a blend of defiance and secrecy. Disturbed by media leaks, he declined to undergo a polygraph test administered by the D.C. police. However, his attorney announced that Condit had passed a lie detector test conducted by a private examiner on July 13. His public demeanor remained enigmatic, particularly during a televised interview with Connie Chung on ABC News' Primetime Thursday on August 23. Condit meticulously avoided direct answers, further fueling public speculation and media frenzy.

This intense media coverage was mirrored by public opinion. A national Fox News/Opinion Dynamics poll conducted in July 2001 revealed a divided America: 44 percent of respondents suspected Condit's involvement in Levy's disappearance, while 27 percent believed he should resign. Over half of the polled participants felt Condit's behavior was indicative of guilt, though only 13 percent supported his re-election. Interestingly, constituents in Condit's congressional district held a more favorable opinion of him.

The Levy controversy, however, cast a long shadow over Condit's political career. In a stunning political defeat, Condit lost the Democratic primary election for his Congressional seat on March 5, 2002, to his former aide, then-Assemblyman Dennis Cardoza, with the Levy case being a significant factor. Condit's involvement with the case continued as he was subpoenaed to appear before a District of Columbia grand jury on April 1, 2002, a date shrouded in secrecy to prevent media leaks. The culmination of this saga saw Condit exiting Congress on January 3, 2003, after his bid for re-election was unsuccessful, a clear testament to the lasting impact of the Chandra Levy case on his political fate.

The search for Chandra Levy, which had held the nation's attention in a grip of mystery and speculation, reached a chilling climax on the morning of May 22, 2002. At approximately 9:30 am, a man walking his dog in Rock Creek Park, a serene natural haven in the heart of Washington, D.C., made a grim discovery. While searching for turtles near Broad Branch Creek, he stumbled upon skeletal remains. These remains, later confirmed through dental records, tragically belonged to Levy.

The scene where Levy's remains were found was a secluded, forested area along a steep incline in the park. Scattered around the site were bones and various personal items, lying exposed, not buried. Among the recovered evidence were a sports bra, sweatshirt, leggings, and tennis shoes - silent testaments to the tragedy that had occurred. This discovery was particularly disconcerting because it was made in a portion of the park that had eluded previous police searches. Despite extensive efforts that covered over half of the park's vast 1,754 acres, this particular wooded slope had remained unexplored. A critical miscommunication had led search teams to focus only within 100 yards of the park's roads, inadvertently missing this crucial area. The remains lay undisturbed, a mere four miles from Levy's apartment, holding the key to the mystery that had perplexed the city and the nation.

The recovery of Levy's remains marked a turning point in the investigation. Following a preliminary autopsy, the District of Columbia police announced the opening of a homicide investigation, a move that confirmed the worst fears about Levy's fate. On May 28, D.C. Medical Examiner Jonathan L. Arden officially declared Levy's death a homicide. However, the passage of time had taken its toll, leaving limited evidence for investigators to work with. Arden noted significant damage to Levy's hyoid bone, a detail that hinted at possible strangulation, but he stopped short of conclusively attributing her death to this cause.

The saga took yet another distressing turn on June 6. After the official police search had concluded, private investigators hired by the Levy family discovered more of her remains. Her shin bone, along with some twisted wire, was found about 25 yards from the primary site where her other remains had been located. This oversight by the police search teams drew sharp criticism, especially from Police Chief Charles H. Ramsey, who publicly expressed his dissatisfaction with the failure to locate these critical pieces of evidence earlier.

On May 28, 2002, the Levy family organized a deeply moving memorial service at the Modesto Centre Plaza. This event, marked by a profound sense of loss and community solidarity, drew an overwhelming crowd of over 1,200 attendees, some of whom traveled from as far as Los Angeles. The 90-minute ceremony saw an outpouring of grief and remembrance, with heartfelt speeches delivered by Levy's brother, grandmother, great-aunt, and close friends. Rabbi Paul Gordon offered a touching eulogy in both Hebrew and English, poignantly describing Levy as "a good person taken from us much too soon."

A year later, on May 27, 2003, a more intimate gathering took place as Levy's remains were laid to rest in Lakewood Memorial Park Cemetery in Hughson, California, close to her hometown of Modesto. Attended by approximately 40 of Levy's friends and family, the private burial ceremony was a moment of closure, marked by the release of 12 white doves, symbolizing peace and the spirit's journey.

Amidst the mourning, the investigation into Levy's death took a dramatic turn in September 2001. Washington, D.C. police and federal prosecutors received a startling claim from the lawyer of an informant, held in D.C. Jail. The informant, whose identity was concealed for his safety, alleged that Ingmar Guandique, a 20-year-old undocumented immigrant from El Salvador also incarcerated in the jail, confessed to him about being hired by Congressman Condit for $25,000 to murder Levy.

However, this narrative soon unraveled. Investigators dismissed the story linking Condit to the crime, especially since Guandique had confessed to assaulting two other women in Rock Creek Park, the same location where Levy's remains were discovered. Adding to the suspicion, Guandique was absent from work on the day Levy disappeared, and his former landlady recalled seeing him with facial scratches and bruises around that time. Despite these connections, the investigators did not interview the other victims of Rock Creek Park assaults.

Police Chief Ramsey cautiously referred to Guandique as a "person of interest" rather than a suspect, urging reporters not to overemphasize his involvement. Assistant Chief Terrance W. Gainer remarked that if Guandique had been a primary suspect, the police would have pursued him aggressively.

Guandique consistently denied any involvement in Levy's attack. In an effort to verify the informant's claim, the FBI administered a polygraph test to him on November 28, which he failed. A subsequent polygraph test on Guandique, conducted on February 4, 2002, yielded inconclusive results but was officially deemed "not deceptive." The language barrier posed a significant challenge in these tests, as neither the informant nor Guandique was fluent in English. Chief Detective Jack Barrett expressed a preference for bilingual examiners, who were unfortunately unavailable at the time.

When Judge Noel Anketell Kramer was questioned about Guandique's possible link to the Levy case, she dismissed it as a "satellite issue" unrelated to the main investigation. Kramer sentenced Guandique to a 10-year prison term for his attacks on the other women in Rock Creek Park. Following his sentencing, Guandique was initially sent to the U.S. Penitentiary, Big Sandy in Kentucky, and later transferred to the U.S. Penitentiary in Victorville, California.

The unsolved mystery lingered as a "cold case" for several years, a testament to the complexity and challenges that had baffled investigators. However, in 2006, a renewed vigor was infused into the investigation with the appointment of Cathy L. Lanier as the new D.C. police chief. Recognizing the need for fresh perspectives and expertise, Lanier decisively replaced the lead detective on the Levy case, bringing in three veteran investigators who possessed a wealth of homicide experience.

In 2007, the investigative narrative took a significant turn. The editors of The Washington Post, sensing that critical aspects of the case remained unexplored, assigned a new team of reporters to delve into the Levy case anew. This dedicated team spent a year meticulously re-examining the intricate details of the case. Their efforts culminated in a series of revealing articles published in the summer of 2008. These articles critically highlighted the initial investigative shortcomings, particularly the failure to thoroughly probe Ingmar Guandique's connection to other attacks in Rock Creek Park.

September 2008 marked another pivotal moment in the investigation. Authorities conducted a meticulous search of Guandique's federal prison cell in California. In a chilling discovery, they found a magazine photo of Levy that Guandique had kept, a piece of evidence that cast new suspicions on him. Further bolstering the case, police conducted interviews with Guandique's acquaintances and witnesses of the previous Rock Creek Park incidents.

The case against Guandique took a formal turn on March 3, 2009, when the Superior Court of the District of Columbia issued an arrest warrant for him. On April 20, he was transferred back to the District of Columbia Department of Corrections, making a brief stop at the Federal Transfer Center in Oklahoma City. Two days later, a dramatic development unfolded as Guandique was officially charged in D.C. with Levy's murder.

The indictment presented against Guandique was extensive and grave. He faced six counts, including kidnapping, first-degree murder committed during a kidnapping, attempted first-degree sexual abuse, first-degree murder committed during a sexual offense, attempted robbery, and first-degree murder committed during a robbery. Guandique, maintaining his innocence, pleaded not guilty at his arraignment. The court initially set a trial date for January 27, 2010, but his lawyers raised a jurisdictional challenge, arguing that the search of Guandique's federal prison cell was beyond the court's authority.

Complications arose as the trial approached. In an unfortunate turn of events, some of the evidence gathered was contaminated with DNA from employees of the prosecution. This mishap necessitated a delay in the trial proceedings. Consequently, the start date was pushed to October 4, 2010, at the H. Carl Moultrie Courthouse.

The trial of Ingmar Guandique for the murder of Chandra Levy commenced with a palpable air of anticipation and gravity on October 18, 2010. In the Superior Court of the District of Columbia, under the watchful eye of Judge Gerald I. Fisher, the complex process of jury selection began. This critical phase set the stage for what was to be a closely watched and high-stakes trial. Assistant U.S. Attorney Fernando Campoamor-Sanchez laid the groundwork for the prosecution's case, unveiling a list of potential witnesses, including the prominent FBI agent Brad Garrett and the two women who had previously been assaulted by Guandique in Rock Creek Park.

The prosecution's strategy and timeline were ambitious. They anticipated their presentation would span approximately four weeks, while the defense's response was expected to take just one day. The trial moved into a dramatic phase on October 25 and 26, when Halle Shilling and Christy Wiegand, the victims of Guandique's previous assaults, took the stand. Their harrowing testimonies recounted the terrifying experiences of being attacked while jogging independently in Rock Creek Park. Wiegand vividly described the chilling moment when Guandique grabbed her from behind, dragged her down a ravine, and menacingly held a knife to her face.

In a deeply emotional moment on October 26, 2010, Chandra Levy's then-64-year-old father, Robert Levy, offered his testimony. He poignantly revisited and revised past statements regarding his suspicions of former Congressman Gary Condit. Robert Levy, reflecting on his initial beliefs, testified that he had previously conveyed to authorities his conviction that his daughter Chandra would have been too cautious to jog alone in the woods. However, he confessed that his views had since changed. He also recounted telling police about an alleged five-year plan between his daughter and Condit, which included marriage. In a moment of candor, he admitted that his earlier accusations against Condit were driven by a desperate need to find a culprit, saying, "I just said whatever came to mind just to point to him as the villain." Levy noted that his perspective shifted dramatically upon learning about Guandique's involvement.

The trial took another significant turn on November 1, when Gary Condit himself testified. Faced with direct questions about the nature of his relationship with Chandra Levy, Condit steadfastly maintained his privacy, responding, "I am not going to respond to that question out of privacy for myself and Chandra." This stance added an element of intrigue and complexity to the trial.

Further complicating matters, FBI biologist Alan Giusti presented evidence that would link Condit to Levy in a different way. He testified that semen found on underwear in Levy's apartment contained sperm matching Condit's DNA profile.

The trial took a dramatic turn with the testimony of prosecution witness Armando Morales. Morales, who had shared a cell with Guandique at the U.S. Penitentiary in Kentucky, provided a riveting account that captivated the courtroom. He recounted that Guandique, a fellow member of the Mara Salvatrucha gang, was anxious about being transferred between prisons in 2006 due to the potential violence against inmates suspected of rape. In a moment of apparent vulnerability, Guandique confided to Morales that he had indeed killed Levy in an attempted robbery, but he vehemently denied raping her.

The prosecution, having woven their narrative, rested their case on November 10. In a strategic move, they dropped two of the six charges against Guandique: the sexual assault and the murder associated with that assault. The defense then took center stage on November 15, resting its case without calling Guandique to testify. They countered Morales' testimony with other prison witnesses. Jose Manuel Alaniz, who had shared a cell with both Guandique and Morales, claimed that Guandique never mentioned rape or murder. Alaniz, under cross-examination, admitted his lack of curiosity about Guandique's conversations and his frequent periods of sleep due to recovery from a gunshot wound. The prosecution further reduced their charges, dropping kidnapping and attempted robbery due to the expiration of the statute of limitations.

The trial reached a crescendo during closing arguments for the remaining charges of first-degree murder committed during a kidnapping and during a robbery. Prosecutor Amanda Haines put forth a harrowing scenario, suggesting Guandique bound and gagged Levy, leaving her to perish from dehydration or exposure in the park. Defense attorney Santha Sonenberg, however, pointed to the glaring absence of DNA evidence linking Guandique to the crime scene. She painted the prosecution's case as "fiction," proposing an alternative theory that Levy was killed elsewhere and her body later disposed of in the park.

Jury deliberations began on November 17, 2010, amidst heightened courthouse security that led to procedural delays. After two days, all but one juror were in favor of convicting Guandique. On the third day, the jury sought clarification from Judge Gerald Fisher on the definition of assault, to which Fisher responded that any physical injury, regardless of its severity, could legally be considered an assault.

On November 22, 2010, the jury delivered their verdict: Guandique was found guilty on both counts of first-degree murder. A juror later revealed that Morales' testimony had been pivotal in reaching this verdict, described by some as a "miracle" given the reliance on circumstantial evidence. Gladys Weatherspoon, Guandique's former attorney in the 2001 assault cases, expressed her dismay at the verdict, reflecting a sentiment of inevitability driven by sympathy for Susan Levy, Chandra's mother, who had been a constant presence in the courtroom.

In the aftermath of the trial, Susan Levy addressed the media, expressing a lingering sadness and dismissing the notion of closure. She has since been active in ensuring that the photographic evidence of her daughter's remains is kept sealed from public view, preserving the dignity of Chandra's memory in the face of ongoing media interest.

On February 1, 2011, Guandique's legal team ignited a new wave of controversy by requesting a new trial. They filed a comprehensive 17-page document, arguing that the jury's verdict was influenced by improper means. The defense contended that the prosecution's approach had unduly swayed the jury's emotions, citing their use of "references to facts not in evidence." Furthermore, they raised concerns about jury conduct, specifically pointing to an allegation that one juror, who refrained from taking notes, had been influenced by another juror's notes, a potential breach of the judge's instructions.

The prosecution firmly opposed the call for a retrial. They argued that the issue regarding the juror's notes was a minor technicality that had no substantial impact on the final verdict. The stakes were high for Guandique, who faced a minimum sentence of 30 years and a potential life imprisonment without parole. The prosecutors, seeking the maximum sentence, portrayed Guandique as a perpetual threat to women, citing his inability to control his actions. Their February 2011 memo painted a disturbing picture of Guandique's behavior in prison, including harassment of female staff, solicitation of a nurse, and inappropriate conduct in front of guards.

Assistant U.S. Attorney Fernando Campoamor-Sanchez revealed an extensive investigation that extended to El Salvador. He traveled there with a detective to probe allegations that Guandique had fled his native country due to suspected attacks against local women dating back to 1999. The sentencing hearing on February 11 was a moment of high drama. Guandique addressed Levy's family, expressing sorrow for what happened to their daughter but maintaining his innocence. A poignant moment ensued when Susan Levy, Chandra's mother, confronted Guandique, seeking a direct admission of guilt. Judge Gerald Fisher, however, denied Guandique's motion for a retrial and imposed a 60-year prison sentence, labeling Guandique a "sexual predator."

In the aftermath, Guandique continued to assert his innocence. His legal battle persisted as his public defender, James Klein, filed an appeal of the conviction with the District of Columbia Court of Appeals on February 25, 2011. The court's procedural timeline suggested a lengthy wait for a resolution, averaging 588 days for appeals.

The case took a secretive turn between December 2012 and January 2013, with a series of confidential hearings that piqued public curiosity. The nature of these meetings remained shrouded in secrecy, as ordered by the judge. It was not until after a third hearing in February that the judge unsealed transcripts from the previous sessions, revealing that Klein was pushing for a new trial based on newfound evidence.

The saga took a dramatic and unexpected turn in May 2015, when prosecutors withdrew their opposition to granting Ingmar Guandique a new trial. This significant development was fueled by defense assertions that the prosecution's key witness, Armando Morales, had committed perjury during his testimony. The defense accused Morales, a jailhouse informant, of fabricating Guandique's confession to curry favor with the prosecutors, despite Morales' claims of never having served as an informant. The credibility of Morales was further questioned due to his reputation for being untrustworthy, an aspect the defense claimed was not adequately disclosed by the prosecution.

In a twist that added more complexity to the case, on June 3, the defense introduced testimony from a new witness. This neighbor had made a chilling 911 call at 4:37 a.m. on the last day Levy was known to be alive, reporting a 'blood-curdling scream' that possibly emanated from Levy's apartment. This revelation prompted Judge Gerald Fisher to approve the motion for a new trial the following day. Judge Robert E. Morin scheduled the retrial for March 1, 2016, but it was subsequently postponed to October 11.

November 2015 brought another revelation when prosecutors admitted to a D.C. Superior Court judge that crucial documents had not been shared with the defense prior to Guandique's first trial. Following this disclosure, in December 2015, the defense filed new court motions, arguing for the dismissal of the charges. This argument hinged on the incomplete disclosure of a memo detailing prosecutors' interactions with Morales. Morales had testified at trial that he had never collaborated with law enforcement before the Levy case. However, the missing page of the memo revealed his previous engagements with law enforcement regarding gang activity, suggesting a potential motive for Morales to tailor his testimony in favor of the prosecution.

The case reached a pivotal moment on July 28, 2016, when prosecutors declared their decision not to proceed with the retrial against Guandique. Instead, they opted to pursue his deportation. This decision came on the heels of a revelation reported by The Washington Post: Morales, now residing in Maryland, had been secretly recorded admitting to lying on the witness stand during the 2010 trial. The recording, made by Babs Proller and subsequently handed over to the police, cast a shadow of doubt over the integrity of Morales' testimony. The U.S. Attorney's Office, citing new information that emerged in the preceding week, concluded that there was insufficient evidence to move forward with the retrial.

In a documentary episode of "An American Murder Mystery" focusing on the case, it was revealed that in March 2017, Guandique's efforts to remain in the United States were unsuccessful. Consequently, in May of the same year, he was deported to his native El Salvador, marking the end of a long, convoluted legal journey that left many questions unanswered.

The actions of prosecutors Fernando Campoamor-Sánchez and Amanda Haines came under intense scrutiny. Defense lawyers for Ingmar Guandique harbored strong suspicions that these prosecutors had intentionally withheld crucial evidence — specifically, the first page of a memo related to key witness Armando Morales. This belief led them to file a formal complaint with the Justice Department's Office of Professional Responsibility (OPR), triggering a thorough investigation that spanned two years. The OPR, after its extensive review, concluded that there were no ethical or legal violations committed by Campoamor-Sánchez and Haines.

Following the controversy, Campoamor-Sánchez transitioned out of the Justice Department to a new role at the Securities and Exchange Commission, while Haines entered retirement. However, the case was far from closed in the legal community. In 2020, the District of Columbia Bar's Office of Disciplinary Counsel (ODC) announced its intention to probe the allegations against the two prosecutors. By May of the following year, charges were formally brought, reigniting the debate over their conduct during the trial.

At the subsequent hearing, both Campoamor-Sánchez and Haines presented their defenses. Haines maintained her belief that the entire memo had been turned over to the defense, suggesting the possibility that the first page was lost by the defense team. She argued that there was no incentive for the prosecution to deliberately withhold the document, as it did not significantly undermine their case. However, Haines acknowledged that she sometimes delayed sharing detailed information about witnesses with the defense, citing past instances where such disclosures had tragically led to witness fatalities.

The hearing also shed light on internal tensions between Campoamor-Sánchez and Haines. They admitted to disagreements over disclosure practices to the defense, a reflection of the lack of clear guidelines within the Justice Department at the time. This lack of clarity extended to their roles in the trial, leading to conflicts over who would question Morales and deliver the closing argument — tasks originally assigned to Campoamor-Sánchez but later taken over by Haines, a move that left him feeling sidelined.

Three months after the hearing, the ODC released a preliminary finding. It concluded that both Campoamor-Sánchez and Haines had breached bar rules mandating the disclosure of potentially exculpatory evidence to defense attorneys. The ODC recommended a six-month suspension from practicing law for both attorneys. This recommendation was met with strong resistance. Haines's lawyer vehemently contested the proposed sanction, describing it as "unhinged—from both reality and from any precedent in law or logic." Throughout these proceedings, both Campoamor-Sánchez and Haines consistently denied any allegations of misconduct.

The ongoing legal saga surrounding the actions of these two prosecutors added yet another layer of complexity to the already convoluted and highly scrutinized Chandra Levy case, illustrating the intricate and often contentious nature of legal ethics and prosecutorial conduct.

2001 Anthrax Attacks

In the shadow of the September 11th tragedy, a sinister series of events unfolded, beginning just a week later. The anthrax attacks, a chilling echo of the recent devastation, swept through the United States in a terrifying two-wave assault. Initially, anthrax-laced letters postmarked from Trenton, New Jersey, dated September 18, 2001, were dispatched to major news outlets and a media company in New York City and Florida. The lethal nature of these letters was tragically confirmed with the death of Robert Stevens, an employee at the Sun tabloid, on October 5, 2001, marking the start of a mysterious and deadly outbreak.

The anthrax, resembling coarse brown granules, claimed its victims silently and indiscriminately. In a subsequent and more alarming wave, two additional letters, postmarked October 9, targeted prominent U.S. Senators Tom Daschle and Patrick Leahy. These letters, filled with a more potent and refined anthrax powder, intensified the fear and uncertainty gripping the nation.

Amidst conflicting reports and investigations, at least 22 individuals fell victim to the anthrax attacks, with 11 suffering from the more severe inhalational form. Tragically, five succumbed to this insidious threat, including postal workers and residents from diverse backgrounds. The protracted and elusive hunt for the perpetrator drew parallels with the infamous Unabomber case, underscoring the elusive and enigmatic nature of these bio-terror attacks.

In a twist that linked the anthrax attacks to the quiet town of Princeton, New

Jersey, investigators honed in on a single mailbox on 10 Nassau Street, near the prestigious Princeton University. This discovery came after a meticulous search involving approximately 600 mailboxes, with the one on Nassau Street emerging as the sole positive for anthrax spores.

The menacing messages enclosed in the letters sent to the New York Post, NBC News, and U.S. Senators Daschle and Leahy were chillingly clear. Each letter was marked with the same date, "09-11-01," symbolically tying them to the September 11 attacks. The notes, crudely advising to take penicillin and declaring death to America and Israel, were underscored by the phrase "ALLAH IS GREAT." These messages not only conveyed threats but also sowed seeds of fear and confusion.

Intriguingly, all the letters were photocopies, their originals never recovered. Each showed subtle differences: varying sizes, punctuation usage, and handwriting styles. The handwriting on the letters sent to the media was noticeably larger than that on the letters sent to the Senators.

Adding to the mystery, the letters addressed to Senators Daschle and Leahy featured a fictitious return address from a non-existent "Greendale School" in Franklin Park, New Jersey, with an incorrect ZIP code.

A host of letters, initially suspected to be linked to the anthrax attacks, later proved to be unrelated, adding layers of confusion to the case.

In the early stages, hoax letters from St. Petersburg, Florida, masqueraded as potential anthrax threats. Adding to the intrigue, a letter received at Microsoft's Reno, Nevada office, initially tested positive for anthrax. This letter, originating from Malaysia, inadvertently drew suspicion towards Steven Hatfill, due to his Malaysian girlfriend, as noted by Marilyn Thompson of The Washington Post. However, it turned out to be a benign package containing only a check and pornography.

The New York Times newsroom was not spared from the hysteria, as reporter Judith Miller received a copycat hoax letter filled with harmless white powder. Similarly, American Media, Inc. in Boca Raton, Florida, already reeling from the anthrax impact, received an odd package addressed to Jennifer Lopez. This package, filled with an eclectic mix of items including a cigar tube and a love letter, was yet another false lead.

Even Senator Daschle's office received a mimic letter from London, coincidentally when Hatfill was in England, sparking more unfounded speculation. Additionally, a dubious letter suggesting Dr. Assaad as a biological terrorist surfaced, but it bore no relation to the anthrax letters.

Amidst this whirlwind of events, Don Foster, a Vassar College English professor, ventured to connect these hoax letters and the anthrax cases to Steven Hatfill, leading to widespread media coverage in Vanity Fair and Reader's Digest. Hatfill, later exonerated, pursued legal action, resulting in an out-of-court settlement.

The letters sent to media organizations contained a coarse brown anthrax material, which primarily caused cutaneous (skin) infections. However, there was an alarming exception: Kathy Nguyen, who contracted the more lethal inhalational anthrax under similar circumstances and in proximity to others affected by the cutaneous form. Intriguingly, the letter responsible for inhalational cases in Florida, addressed to American Media, Inc., was mailed concurrently with the other media-targeted letters.

In contrast, the anthrax mailed to Senators Daschle and Leahy was a fine powder, predominantly resulting in inhalational anthrax cases. Remarkably, two individuals, postal worker Patrick O'Donnell and accountant Linda Burch, contracted the less severe cutaneous anthrax from these Senate letters.

A pivotal discovery was that all the anthrax used in these attacks originated from the same bacterial strain, known as the Ames strain. Despite its name suggesting a connection to Ames, Iowa, the strain was actually isolated from a cow in Texas in 1981, and the "Ames" label resulted from a labeling mix-up. The Ames strain, first studied at the US Army Medical Research Institute of Infectious Diseases in Maryland, had been distributed to several research labs across the United States and internationally.

To unravel this biological mystery, DNA sequencing of the anthrax from the first victim, Robert Stevens, was initiated at The Institute for Genomic Research in December 2001. The swift completion of this sequencing led to findings published in the journal "Science" by early 2002.

Furthermore, radiocarbon dating by the Lawrence Livermore National Laboratory pinpointed the age of the anthrax spores, revealing they were cultured no more than two years prior to the mailings.

In early 2002, a significant development emerged. Scientists at The Institute for Genomic Research (TIGR) discovered variants or mutations in the anthrax cultures from the letters' powder. Between 2002 and 2004, they sequenced the genomes of these isolates, identifying three substantial DNA changes. Each change involved either a duplication or triplication of DNA regions, ranging from 823 to 2607 base pairs, all near the same genes. These findings, published in the Proceedings of the National Academy of Sciences in 2011, formed the foundation for PCR assays. These assays were meticulously validated over the years to test other samples for the same mutations, aiding in building a comprehensive Ames strain repository.

By 2006, the repository contained 1,070 Ames samples, all thoroughly screened. This meticulous process led the FBI to conclude that the anthrax spore powder originated from a specific flask, RMR-1029, under the sole control of scientist Ivins.

A pivotal moment in the investigation occurred on October 24, 2001, when USAMRIID scientist Peter Jahrling reported to the White House potential evidence of silicon in the anthrax from the Daschle letter, suggesting an additive to enhance lung penetration. However, in 2008, Jahrling expressed regret, believing he had made a mistake in his initial assessment.

Richard Preston's book "The Demon in the Freezer" chronicles key events and thoughts of USAMRIID scientists during the critical period of October 16-25, 2001. The book details their initial fears of smallpox contamination and their subsequent discovery of additives in the anthrax spores. The scientists observed an unusual substance boiling off the spores under the microscope, prompting speculation about its sophisticated composition and possible origins from a national bioweapons program or groups like al-Qaeda.

On October 25, 2001, following the White House briefing on the anthrax additives, USAMRIID's Tom Geisbert took a different sample to the Armed Forces Institute of Pathology. There, an X-ray spectrometer revealed the presence of silicon and oxygen – indicating the spores contained silicon dioxide or powdered glass. This finding suggested that the anthrax had been deliberately enhanced, making it more dangerous and effective as a bioweapon.

A significant point of contention arose from the observations made by Peter Jahrling, who initially believed he saw a "goop" oozing from the spores, suggesting an additive. However, this observation was not replicated when different, irradiated spores were examined by the Armed Forces Institute of Pathology (AFIP).

The day after a crucial White House meeting, major newspapers like The New York Times and The Washington Post reported on the potential high-grade nature of the anthrax and the possibility of it being altered with additives to increase its lethality. These reports sparked widespread media speculation over the next eight years, with various news stories discussing the supposed additives in the anthrax spores.

Contrasting these reports, the FBI later posited that the anthrax could have been produced by a single individual with a modest budget and standard lab equipment. This claim was supported by press reports suggesting that the Senate anthrax contained special coatings and additives. Newsweek, for instance, reported on a chemical compound in the Leahy letter's anthrax that was unfamiliar to bioweapons experts.

Amidst these speculations, bioweapons consultants Kenneth Alibek and Matthew Meselson, after reviewing electron micrographs of the anthrax from the Daschle letter, found no evidence of fumed silica coating the spores, challenging earlier assertions.

The debate extended into the scientific community, with one group of scientists in Science magazine suggesting that the anthrax could have been produced with basic lab equipment, while another group described it as a "diabolical advance in biological weapons technology," involving techniques like anchoring silica nanoparticles to spores.

However, in 2006, Douglas Beecher from the FBI's Quantico labs published an article in Applied and Environmental Microbiology. He stated that the anthrax powders were simply spores purified to varying degrees, challenging the notion of additives and sophisticated engineering. Beecher's article criticized the misconception of the spores being produced with advanced techniques akin to military weapon production, arguing that this belief detracted from the real hazards posed by simple spore preparations. Critics of Beecher's article, however, pointed out the lack of supporting references.

ABC's chief investigative correspondent, Brian Ross, stirred controversy by suggesting a link between the anthrax samples and Saddam Hussein, the then-President of Iraq. Ross's claim, made in late October 2001, centered around the alleged presence of bentonite in the anthrax. On October 26, he reported that sources indicated the anthrax sent to Senate Majority Leader Tom Daschle was laced with bentonite, a substance purportedly used exclusively by Iraq in its biochemical weapons. He asserted that the presence of bentonite, determined through tests at Fort Detrick and other locations, was a signature of Hussein's biological weapons program.

This claim was further emphasized on October 28 when Ross reiterated that despite White House denials, sources at Fort Detrick had found traces of bentonite and silica in the anthrax. This narrative was repeated several times over the next couple of days.

However, the White House countered these reports. On October 29, White House spokesperson Scott Stanzel refuted the presence of bentonite in the anthrax samples, stating that no such substance was found based on their tests. On the same day, Major General John Parker, during a White House briefing, acknowledged the discovery of silica in the samples but emphasized the absence of aluminum, a key component of bentonite.

Further clarification came on November 7 from Homeland Security Advisor Tom Ridge, who mentioned that the ingredient in question was silicon, not bentonite. Despite the initial claims by Ross and his reference to "four well-placed and separate sources," there was no subsequent pursuit of the bentonite angle in the public domain, marking a quiet end to the controversy stirred by the initial report.

Analysis showed that a significant proportion (65–75%) of the spores contained silicon within their spore coats. This finding was crucial because it suggested that the silicon was a natural component of the spores, not an additive introduced post-formation, indicating that the spores were not deliberately "weaponized."

In 2010, a Japanese study shed light on the role of silicon in bacteria, revealing that silicon is a "quasiessential" element for many living organisms and can constitute a substantial part of the dry weight in some bacterial spores. This study aligned with observations that certain Bacillus species, closely related to Bacillus anthracis (the bacterium responsible for anthrax), naturally accumulate significant levels of silicon. This natural accumulation led experts like Peter Setlow to speculate that silicon might contribute to the structural rigidity of the spores.

However, the high silicon content in the Leahy letter's powder, pegged at 1.4% by the FBI lab, raised eyebrows. Expert Stuart Jacobson remarked on the unusually high proportion, suggesting it was indicative of deliberate weaponization, a view not commonly observed in cases of accidental contamination.

To investigate further, scientists at Lawrence Livermore National Laboratory conducted experiments to understand if the growth medium's silicon levels influenced the spores' silicon content. Despite numerous attempts, they could not replicate the high silicon levels found in the attack anthrax, leading to the conclusion that factors other than the growth medium's silicon level determined the spores' silicon uptake.

Adding to the complexity, Richard O. Spertzel, a microbiologist and former leader of the United Nations' biological weapons inspections in Iraq, contested the FBI's claim that the anthrax could have originated from the lab where Ivins worked. He cited the high silica levels as evidence of sophisticated processing beyond the capabilities of Ivins' lab.

Jeffrey Adamovicz, who supervised Ivins at Fort Detrick, also doubted the FBI's conclusions, asserting that the high silicon content must have been an added component. He noted that their facility lacked the equipment, such as a large fermentor, which could introduce silicon to anthrax spores.

In a dramatic turn, some concluded that the anthrax might have been produced by a US-based pharmaceutical company, possibly contracted by the government. This theory suggested a motive to garner support for the war in Iraq, though it remains a contentious and unverified claim.

The exhaustive and global investigation into the anthrax attacks, known as Amerithrax, represented a monumental effort by authorities. Teams journeyed across six continents, interviewing over 9,000 individuals, executing 67 search operations, and issuing more than 6,000 subpoenas. In the initial stages, the FBI deployed hundreds of personnel, grappling with the possibility of a link between the September 11 al-Qaeda attacks and the anthrax incidents, a connection they eventually ruled out. As late as September 2006, the case still engaged 17 FBI agents and 10 postal inspectors, with FBI Special Agent C. Frank Figliuzzi leading the evidence recovery operations.

A significant setback in the investigation occurred with the destruction of a vital anthrax spore collection at Iowa State University. With authorization from the FBI and the Centers for Disease Control and Prevention (CDC), the university destroyed its extensive anthrax archive on October 10 and 11, 2001. This collection, amassed over seven decades and comprising over 100 vials of anthrax spores, was considered potentially crucial evidence. The loss of this collection deprived investigators of genetic clues that might have linked the anthrax used in the attacks to a specific strain, potentially narrowing down the perpetrator's identity.

The anthrax attacks also prompted intense pressure from the White House on FBI Director Robert Mueller to attribute the attacks to al-Qaeda, especially following the September 11 incidents. Mueller faced significant pressure during intelligence briefings to establish a connection to Osama bin Laden, reflecting a strong inclination to implicate Middle Eastern actors. President Bush and Vice President Cheney echoed these suspicions in their public statements, fueling speculation about al-Qaeda's involvement.

Amidst this climate, media outlets like The Guardian, The Wall Street Journal, and ABC News contributed to the narrative linking the attacks to Iraq and al-Qaeda. These reports often cited the alleged presence of bentonite in the anthrax, suggesting Iraqi involvement. However, this narrative was eventually debunked, as no bentonite was ever found in the anthrax samples.

Despite the correction, the initial reports had a lasting impact, with some journalists continuing to reference the discredited bentonite claim, even after the invasion of Iraq disproved any Iraqi involvement in the attacks.

Barbara Hatch Rosenberg, a molecular biologist and chair of a biological weapons panel at the Federation of American Scientists, emerged as a vocal proponent of the theory that the attacks were the work of an insider, possibly a "rogue CIA agent." This theory gained traction when it was revealed that the Ames strain of anthrax was used in the attacks. Rosenberg informed the FBI of her suspicions and named the person she considered "most likely" responsible.

Rosenberg's claims gained wider attention as she published documents and gave speeches outlining her theory. In December 2001, she suggested on the Federation of American Scientists' website that the attacks were carried out with the help of a sophisticated government program. Her views were echoed in a January 2002 column by Nicholas Kristof in The New York Times, sparking widespread media interest.

However, the FBI did not endorse Rosenberg's theory, stating they had no prime suspect at the time. Her claims were also discounted by other FBI officials. Despite this, Rosenberg continued to present her theories, including to senate staffers working for Senators Daschle and Leahy.

Around this time, Steven Hatfill, a virologist, became a focus of the investigation. The FBI's search of his apartment in June 2002 thrust him into the public eye, though he was not officially declared a suspect. Subsequent media reports frequently mentioned Hatfill in relation to the case.

In August 2002, Attorney General John Ashcroft named Hatfill as a "person of interest," but no charges were filed against him. Hatfill consistently denied involvement in the anthrax attacks and eventually sued various parties, including the FBI, the Justice Department, and several media outlets, for defamation and violation of his constitutional rights.

Hatfill's legal battles were significant. While his lawsuit against The New York Times was initially dismissed, it was later reinstated on appeal before being ultimately upheld due to the failure to prove malice. The Supreme Court declined to hear his appeal. His lawsuits against Vanity Fair, Reader's Digest, and Vassar College were settled out of court, though the details were not disclosed.

The Department of Justice agreed to settle Hatfill's case for $5.8 million in June 2008.

Bruce E. Ivins, a biodefense researcher at Fort Detrick's government bio-defense labs for 18 years, became a central figure in the Amerithrax investigation. His apparent suicide in August 2008, at the age of 62, came amid reports that the FBI was preparing to charge him in connection with the anthrax attacks. However, the evidence against him was primarily circumstantial, and the grand jury in Washington was reportedly not ready to issue an indictment at the time of his death. This development prompted Rush D. Holt Jr., who represented the district where the anthrax letters were mailed, to call for a more thorough examination of the evidence and the FBI's investigation.

Questions about Ivins' capability to weaponize anthrax into an inhalable powder were raised by scientists familiar with germ warfare. Alan Zelicoff, who assisted the FBI, expressed skepticism about Ivins' ability to carry out such sophisticated work, noting that aerosol physics, not biology, would be required.

Colleagues at Fort Detrick described the immense pressure Ivins faced during the investigation. W. Russell Byrne, who worked in the same facility, noted that Ivins was "hounded" by FBI agents and had been hospitalized for depression. Byrne described Ivins as psychologically exhausted but not a "ticking bomb."

In August 2008, federal prosecutors posthumously named Ivins as the sole perpetrator, citing evidence that the anthrax spores originated from a strain maintained by him. However, this claim was met with skepticism from experts like Meryl Nass, who argued that microbial forensics could link the anthrax to a specific strain and lab but not definitively to an individual. The investigation had identified over 400 people who had access to the anthrax strain or the lab where it was stored.

Disturbing revelations about Ivins' mental state emerged from his interactions with mental health professionals. In 2000, a counselor reported Ivins' detailed homicidal plan towards a young woman, which he had shared in a disturbingly emotionless manner. Ivins' psychiatrist, Dr. David Irwin, later described him as "homicidal, sociopathic with clear intentions," and another therapist reported in 2008 that Ivins had expressed plans to kill his co-workers.

The Department of Justice's report on the Amerithrax investigation painted a picture of Bruce E. Ivins as a man whose actions and statements suggested a consciousness of guilt. The report highlighted several instances of Ivins' behavior that raised suspicion: he took unauthorized environmental samples in his lab and decontaminated areas he worked in without reporting, discarded a book on secret codes similar to those used in the anthrax letters, threatened other scientists, made ambiguous comments about his involvement, and attempted to divert suspicion towards others.

The FBI found contradictions in Ivins' explanations for his actions, particularly regarding the environmental sampling and subsequent activities. Central to the case was flask RMR-1029, controlled by Ivins, which the Department of Justice claimed was used to create the anthrax used in the attacks.

In 2002, the possibility of using DNA sequencing to distinguish anthrax variants was a novel idea, and Ivins suggested this approach to the FBI. Despite skepticism from other researchers, he educated FBI agents on identifying genetic mutations in anthrax. Ivins voluntarily provided samples from his Ames strain collection, including two from flask RMR-1029. However, these samples were reportedly in the wrong type of test tube, rendering them inadmissible in court. When informed that his samples didn't meet FBI requirements, Ivins prepared new samples, but these did not match the mutations later identified in flask RMR-1029.

In April 2004, when colleague Henry Heine discovered a test tube of anthrax, Ivins suggested it might be from RMR-1029 and advised Heine to send a sample to the FBI. This incident led to doubts about the FBI's testing reliability, as one sample tested negative and another positive.

A DOJ summary report from 2010 suggested that Ivins may have obstructed the investigation by providing false samples. Records released in 2011 showed that Ivins provided four sets of samples between 2002 and 2004, with three sets testing positive for the targeted morphs, contrary to the FBI's earlier report.

In a group therapy session in July 2008, Ivins expressed intense anger towards the investigators, the government, and the system. He revealed his status as a suspect in the anthrax investigation and mentioned a plan to harm co-workers and others, boasting about his ability to commit murder without leaving evidence. He also mentioned owning a bullet-proof vest and planning to acquire a Glock firearm from his son.

According to the FBI's analysis of the letters sent to the media during the anthrax attacks, there appeared to be a pattern where the letters 'A' and 'T' were sometimes emphasized, possibly indicating a hidden code. This observation was based on the apparent emboldening of these characters in the text of the letters.

In their investigation, the FBI found potential significance in this pattern following a search of Bruce Ivins' home, cars, and office on November 1, 2007. Their interest was further piqued when, a week later, they observed Ivins discarding specific items in his trash. Among these were a copy of the book "Gödel, Escher, Bach: An Eternal Golden Braid" by Douglas Hofstadter, known for its exploration of encoding and decoding procedures, including the concept of hiding a message within a message by emphasizing certain characters.

The FBI's scrutiny also extended to a 1992 issue of "American Scientist Journal," which featured an article discussing, among other topics, codons and hidden messages in DNA. This discovery aligned with the highlighted characters in the anthrax letters.

Upon further analysis, the FBI extracted the sequences 'TTT', 'AAT', and 'TAT' from the emboldened letters in the anthrax letters. In biochemical terms, these sequences are codons, each representing a specific amino acid.

From this, two potential hidden meanings were suggested: 'FNY', possibly a verbal assault on New York, and 'PAT', which could refer to a colleague of Ivins. This interpretation was speculative, and the FBI report acknowledged the impossibility of determining the exact meaning of these sequences. However, they emphasized the significance of the presence of a hidden message, rather than its specific interpretation. The report also noted Ivins' known interest in codes and hidden messages and his familiarity with biochemical codons.

The mailings were marked by several indications suggesting that the sender might have been more interested in issuing a warning rather than causing actual harm. Notably, none of the primary recipients of the letters became infected, which points towards a possibility that the sender did not intend for the anthrax to infect these individuals. Additionally, the envelopes used in the mailings were carefully taped over at the seams, an action that could be interpreted as an effort to prevent the anthrax powder from escaping. This attention to detail was further evident in the way the letters were folded. The "pharmaceutical fold" used, historically a method for safely transporting powdered substances, was indicative of an attempt to securely contain the anthrax.

Moreover, the content of the letters themselves hinted at a warning. The letters to media outlets included a specific directive: "TAKE PENACILIN [sic] NOW," which could be seen as a form of precautionary medical advice. In the letters sent to the Senate, the explicit statement, "WE HAVE THIS ANTHRAX," served as a clear alert to the nature of the threat. Furthermore, prevailing beliefs at the time suggested that such powders couldn't escape a sealed envelope except through the corners typically opened by a letter opener, which had been deliberately sealed in these cases.

In June 2008, the focus on Bruce Ivins, who was then involuntarily committed to a psychiatric hospital, added a layer of complexity to the investigation. During a group therapy session, Ivins's statements about the anthrax attacks were described by the FBI as "non-denial denials." He spoke of memory loss and insisted on his non-violent nature, asserting that he lacked both the intent and the technical know-how to create a bio-weapon. He also expressed a general aversion to causing harm, even accidentally, and acknowledged a sense of responsibility due to the security oversight of the anthrax spores at his lab. In January 2008, a confidential source reported to the FBI that Ivins had sporadically claimed at work that he could not intentionally harm or kill someone.

Following the FBI's announcement that Bruce Ivins acted alone in the 2001 anthrax attacks, a wave of skepticism arose from various quarters, including some of Ivins' colleagues and individuals across the political spectrum. Doubts were fueled by several factors, including the fact that Ivins was only one among about a hundred people with access to the particular anthrax vial used in the attacks. Additionally, the FBI could not conclusively place Ivins near the New Jersey mailbox where the anthrax letters were mailed.

Claire Fraser-Ligget, the FBI's genetic consultant, pointed out a significant gap in the case: the absence of any anthrax spores in Ivins' house, vehicle, or personal belongings, which cast doubt on the FBI's conclusions. Jeffrey Adamovicz, who supervised Ivins at USAMRIID's bacteriology division, noted that many at Fort Detrick believed Ivins was innocent, citing unanswered questions about the FBI's scientific methods and the lack of independent peer review of their findings. Over 200 of Ivins' colleagues attended his memorial service, indicating a level of support or disbelief in the FBI's conclusion.

Several alternative theories emerged in the wake of the FBI's announcement. Some suggested FBI incompetence or involvement by foreign entities like Syria or Iraq, and others drew parallels with 9/11 conspiracy theories, suggesting possible foreknowledge of the attacks by the U.S. government. Senator Patrick Leahy, a recipient of one of the anthrax-tainted letters, expressed skepticism about the FBI's evidence, and The Washington Post advocated for an independent investigation due to the case's unresolved aspects.

Senator Leahy, during a Judiciary Committee testimony, directly challenged the FBI's conclusion, stating his belief that others were involved in the attacks, either before or after the fact. In contrast, Tom Daschle, another Democratic senator targeted by the anthrax letters, believed that Ivins was the sole perpetrator.

A key scientific contention in the case was the mismatch between the silicon chemical "fingerprint" of the spores in Ivins' flask RMR-1029 and the spores found in the attack letters. This discrepancy suggested that the spores from the flask had been used to cultivate new spores for the mailings.

On April 22, 2010, the National Research Council, an arm of the National Academy of Sciences, convened a review committee that heard testimony from Henry Heine, a former microbiologist at the Army's biodefense laboratory in Maryland, where Bruce Ivins had worked. Heine challenged the FBI's assertion that Ivins produced the anthrax spores used in the 2001 attacks in his laboratory without detection. Heine argued that producing the quantity of spores found in the letters would have required at least a year of intensive work with the lab's equipment, an effort unlikely to go unnoticed by other lab personnel. He also highlighted that the lab's containment measures were insufficient to prevent the escape of anthrax spores, which would have likely resulted in contamination and illness.

Contrasting views were presented by other scientists. Adam Driks of Loyola University suggested that the anthrax amount in the letters could be produced in just a few days, and emails from Ivins himself indicated a capability of producing large quantities of spores. The New York Times reported that the anthrax powder in the Leahy letter amounted to approximately 871 billion spores.

In a 2011 Journal of Bioterrorism & Biodefense article, three scientists posited that the spore preparation required sophisticated processing, challenging the federal authorities' stance on the simplicity of the material's production. They focused on the high levels of tin found in the anthrax, suggesting that it was used to encapsulate the spores, a technique not feasible in the labs available to Ivins. This finding led to speculation that Ivins might not have acted alone or been the perpetrator. However, Jonathan L. Kiel, a retired Air Force scientist, disagreed, suggesting the tin could be a random contaminant from metal lab containers.

In 2011, Patricia Worsham, then-chief of the Bacteriology Division at the Army lab, stated that the facility lacked the necessary equipment in 2001 to produce the type of spores found in the letters. The government later conceded that the required equipment was not present in the lab, casting doubt on the FBI's claim that Ivins produced the anthrax there. Ivins' colleagues also maintained that it would have been impossible for him to grow the anthrax quantities used in the letters without detection.

Despite these conflicting views and new findings, a spokesperson for the

Justice Department reaffirmed the investigators' belief that Ivins acted alone in the anthrax attacks.

Congressman Rush Holt, representing a district in New Jersey that included a mailbox believed to have been used for mailing the anthrax letters, advocated for a thorough examination of the anthrax attacks. He proposed legislation, the Anthrax Attacks Investigation Act (H.R. 1248), to initiate either a Congressional or an independent commission investigation. This call for an independent inquiry was echoed by other members of Congress.

In contrast, in March 2010, an official from the U.S. administration indicated that President Barack Obama might veto any legislation mandating a new investigation into the 2001 anthrax attacks if it was included in the authorization for the U.S. intelligence agencies' budget. This stance was based on the belief that another investigation could diminish public confidence in the FBI's initial probe. Peter Orszag, then-director of the Office of Management and Budget, expressed concerns in a letter to congressional leaders about the redundancy of such an investigation and the implications of Congress commissioning an agency Inspector General to replicate a criminal investigation.

In what seemed to be a response to ongoing skepticism, the FBI requested an independent review of its scientific findings from the National Academy of Sciences (NAS) on September 16, 2008. FBI Director Mueller had already stated that the scientific methods used in the investigation had been validated through engagement with numerous nonagency scientists.

The NAS review began on April 24, 2009, focusing on the facts and data of the 2001 Bacillus anthracis mailings investigation, as well as the principles and methods used by the FBI. However, the NAS committee was not tasked with assessing the scientific evidence's probative value in any specific aspect of the investigation or legal proceedings, nor were they to comment on the guilt or innocence of individuals involved.

Throughout mid-2009, the NAS committee conducted public sessions with presentations from scientists, including those from the FBI laboratories. In these sessions, key findings were presented, including the absence of silica particles on the outside of the spores, indicating no "weaponization," and the discovery that only some spores in the anthrax letters contained silicon within their spore coats.

In October 2010, the FBI provided additional materials to NAS, including analyses of environmental samples from an overseas location that showed evidence of the Ames strain. The NAS recommended reviewing these investigations.

The NAS committee's report, released on February 15, 2011, concluded that based on the scientific evidence available, it was impossible to definitively ascertain the origins of the anthrax in the letters. The report also questioned the FBI and U.S. Justice Department's conclusion that the anthrax spores in the letters originated from a single batch maintained by Ivins at Fort Detrick. This finding cast further doubt on the FBI's assertion that Ivins was the sole perpetrator.

The anthrax mailings in 2001 resulted in the contamination of numerous buildings, necessitating extensive cleanup efforts. In New York City, buildings including the ABC Headquarters and a Rockefeller Center building housing the New York Post and Fox News were decontaminated by Bio Recovery Corporation and Ohio-based Bio-Recovery Services of America. These companies employed various tools and techniques for the cleanup, such as HEPA filtered air scrubbers, HEPA vacuums, respirators, cyclone foggers, and decontamination foam licensed by Sandia National Laboratories. A significant amount of anthrax-contaminated mail, totaling 93 bags, was removed from the New York Post office alone.

The cleanup of the Brentwood postal facility was a lengthy and expensive process, taking 26 months and costing $130 million. The Hamilton, New

Jersey, postal facility remained closed until March 2005, with its cleanup amounting to $65 million.

The Hart Senate Office Building, where Senate Majority Leader Tom Daschle's office was located, and other locations around Capitol Hill were cleaned up in a collaborative effort led by the United States Environmental Protection Agency. This effort cost $27 million from its Superfund program. An FBI document estimated the total damage from the attacks to exceed $1 billion.

In response to the anthrax attacks and the September 11 attacks, the U.S. government significantly increased funding for biological warfare research and preparedness. The National Institute of Allergy and Infectious Diseases saw a $1.5 billion increase in biowarfare-related funding in 2003. The Project Bioshield Act, passed by Congress in 2004, allocated $5.6 billion over ten years for new vaccines and drugs, including raxibacumab for treating anthrax and an Anthrax Vaccine Adsorbed, both stockpiled by the government.

Following 9/11, and before the anthrax letters were mailed, the White House began distributing ciprofloxacin, the only drug approved by the FDA for inhalational anthrax, to senior staffers. Bayer, the manufacturer of ciprofloxacin, agreed to provide 100,000 doses at a reduced price to the U.S. government after facing potential patent override threats. However, doxycycline was later recommended as a more appropriate treatment for anthrax exposure. The increased use of ciprofloxacin raised concerns about the potential development of drug-resistant bacteria strains. Additionally, several corporations offered to supply drugs for anthrax treatment free or at cost, pending FDA approval for their products. These companies included Bristol Myers Squibb, Johnson and Johnson, GlaxoSmithKline, Eli Lilly, and Pfizer.

Killing of Geetha Angara

Born in the vibrant city of Chennai, India, in 1961, the life journey of Angara is a tale of remarkable academic and personal achievements. She blazed a trail at Loyola College in Chennai, becoming the first woman in the institution's history to earn both bachelor's and master's degrees in chemistry. Her academic prowess was unparalleled, culminating in her being awarded a gold medal as the top student in her class.

In 1984, with a spirit of adventure and ambition, Angara embarked on a new chapter in her life, emigrating to the United States. There, she continued her impressive academic journey, earning additional master's degrees and a doctorate in organic chemistry from the prestigious New York University. This period marked a significant expansion of her expertise and knowledge in her field.

Angara's personal life flourished alongside her academic career. She married a fellow Indian émigré, a professional in the banking sector, and together they started a family, welcoming their first child shortly thereafter. The couple initially made their home in Clifton, New Jersey, a picturesque suburb in Passaic County, where they began building their life together.

Professionally, Angara's journey took her to Merck, where she spent a year analyzing compounds. In 1992, she made a pivotal career move to the Passaic Valley Water Commission (PVWC), a public utility jointly owned by Clifton and the neighboring cities of Passaic and Paterson. This significant role involved overseeing the provision of water to an astounding 800,000 customers across several communities in North Jersey, a testament to her skills and dedication.

Seven years after joining PVWC, Angara and her family relocated to Holmdel, a community 42 miles south in Monmouth County. This move was motivated by the family's desire for a better education system for their children, highlighting Angara's role as not just a career-oriented individual but also a dedicated mother prioritizing her family's wellbeing.

Angara's professional journey at the Passaic Valley Water Commission was marked by both challenges and triumphs. While contemplating the possibility of leaving PVWC, fate had a different plan for her. A significant turning point in her career came when she was promoted to the esteemed position of senior chemist at the plant and, notably, earned a plant operator's license. These achievements were a testament to her dedication and expertise in the field.

In her new role, Angara took on a pivotal responsibility—the transition of the Totowa plant's water purification process from chlorination to an innovative ozone-based method. Her leadership in this ambitious project was a source of great pride, underscoring her commitment to advancing water treatment technology. However, this transformation was not without its challenges, as some of her colleagues harbored resentment towards both her promotion and the switch to the new process. Her husband later recalled the mixed emotions that surrounded her achievements.

Angara's approach to her professional life was characterized by her unwavering focus on her work. While she maintained close working relationships with a select few colleagues, she chose not to engage extensively in socializing with the broader workforce. Her dedication to her craft took precedence, and she remained resolute in her pursuit of excellence.

In the summer of 2004, a minor setback occurred when the newly implemented ozone system experienced a temporary failure, attributed to welding issues. This incident highlighted the intricacies and challenges associated with implementing cutting-edge technology in a critical infrastructure like water treatment.

In a twist of fate, in late January 2005, an unexpected development occurred in Angara's absence from work. A pinkish substance was discovered in the treated water, causing heightened tensions within the PVWC workplace. As a result, Angara was tasked with retraining some of her coworkers, adding an additional layer of complexity to her role.

Notably, Angara had embarked on the process of applying for another license, a decision that further fueled antipathy among certain coworkers who harbored animosity towards her. Sadly, it became evident that some of this negativity was rooted in racial bias. As one coworker later disclosed, a significant portion of the plant's workforce was predominantly white, and the success of an immigrant like Angara seemed to have ruffled a few feathers.

On a crisp February morning, the story of Angara unfolds with a blend of routine and unexpected mysteries. At 7:30 a.m., Angara, a dedicated worker at the plant, began her day with a focused determination. Her morning was structured and purposeful, as she diligently tended to her responsibilities until a brief pause at 9:45 a.m. for breakfast with her close-knit team of coworkers. It was during this casual gathering that a subordinate, noting the precision of their operations, brought to Angara's attention the need for recalibrating the plant's filters and clarity sensors. This suggestion, far from being arbitrary, was rooted in the recent records of the plant's performance.

By 10 a.m., the group dispersed, embarking on their various tasks, with Angara heading back to her usual workspace at 10:30. She was seen equipped for a day of science and communication: a clipboard in hand, a beaker suggesting experiments or tests, and a two-way radio to stay connected. A half-planned meal, a sandwich on her desk, hinted at her intention to return shortly after completing a familiar task.

However, that return never happened. The last glimpse of Angara was as she set out to accomplish what was perceived as a routine job. Concerns began to arise when, around 11 a.m., the same subordinate who had raised the initial suggestion found themselves navigating the basement, only to discover disconcerting signs - broken glass scattered on the floor. This discovery prompted a search, and soon, Angara's unexpected absence became a subject of concern among her colleagues.

The gravity of the situation escalated as the day wore on. Angara's car remained untouched in the parking lot, noticed by a night shift worker at 9:20 p.m., and her personal belongings - the uneaten sandwich and her coat - were left as if frozen in time. Her family, too, sensed something amiss when repeated calls to her cell phone went unanswered, especially troubling as she was due to drive her daughter to a basketball game.

By nightfall, the plant transformed into a search ground with worried coworkers and authorities scanning every corner. The basement, where the subordinate had earlier found broken glass, revealed a more alarming clue. A large aluminum floor panel, typically secured by screws, was found ajar, suggesting some disturbance. Nearby, shards of glass, possibly from Angara's beaker, were found and hastily cleared away, not yet seen as pieces of a larger, more ominous puzzle.

In the early hours of February 9, the plant's operations came to a halt. Officials, driven by the urgency of the situation, decided to drain the tank beneath the misplaced panel. This decision led to the heart-wrenching discovery of Angara's radio and clipboard, and eventually, her own body, tragically located in a different tank. As the day unfolded, the search extended to other tanks, revealing the full extent of the calamity.

In response to this tragic turn of events, the plant issued a precautionary boil-water order to its customers, reflecting a deep-seated concern for public safety even amidst the turmoil. The story of Angara, marked by its routine start and mysterious, tragic end, leaves a lingering sense of sorrow and unanswered questions.

The autopsy performed by pathologists brought to light that Angara was still breathing when she entered the water, tragically concluding her life by drowning. However, the revelations were far more sinister. Deep bruises adorning her neck painted a picture of a possible strangulation attempt preceding her death. Additional bruises found on her waist and elbow spoke silently of a struggle, perhaps a desperate fight for life.

In a significant turn of events, six days after the grim discovery, county prosecutor James Avigliano escalated the case, announcing an investigation into Angara's death as a homicide. This announcement shifted the narrative from a tragic accident to a calculated act of violence.

Detectives began weaving together a theory of the crime, hypothesizing that Angara's assailant first incapacitated her – possibly through strangulation, or as some accounts suggest, a blow to the head with nothing more than bare hands. The next act in this macabre scene involved the assailant opening the access panel to the tank, disposing of Angara's body, and then hurriedly replacing the panel in an attempt to conceal their heinous act. Adding to the complexity, an alarm system designed to detect significant water displacement was found to be non-functional, a detail that might have offered clues had it been working.

The setting of this dark tale was equally daunting. The tank, unlit and devoid of any ladder, presented an insurmountable gap of 5 feet between the water surface and the basement floor. The water, chilling at 36 °F, filled the tank to a depth of 35 feet, offering no refuge or standing place.

Forensic investigation faced formidable challenges. Angara's body, having been submerged for over a day in heavily chlorinated water, was bereft of any trace evidence such as DNA or fingerprints that might have clung to it or her clothing during her final moments. Compounding the loss of potential evidence, the glass fragments from the beaker, possibly a key piece of the puzzle, had been carelessly discarded and lost forever.

The investigation was further hampered by the inadvertent contamination of the crime scene. Before Angara's body was discovered, numerous individuals, including firefighters, police officers, and plant workers, had traversed the area, unknowingly compromising its integrity. The absence of security cameras in the basement area above the tanks, an area typically surveyed by numerous cameras in other parts of the plant, posed an additional challenge. Moreover, the loud machinery characteristic of the area where Angara met her fate would have easily muffled any sounds of a struggle, screams, or the shattering of glass, further cloaking the incident in mystery and silence.

The facility, accessible only via a single driveway, was closely monitored by a dedicated security post. Every individual entering the premises had to undergo a check-in procedure, captured by a surveillance camera. Once inside, however, the cleared individuals could roam the complex with relative freedom. Apart from the south side, which bordered the Passaic River, the rest of the property was securely fenced, limiting unauthorized access.

The security records from the day of the incident painted a clear picture: no one unauthorised had entered the complex. Among the plant's 83 employees, only 50 were present that day. This fact alone significantly narrowed down the list of potential suspects for the police, leading them to believe that Angara's killer was among those present.

The police meticulously combed through potential motives for the crime. The autopsy's revelation that Angara had not suffered sexual assault allowed them to discount that as a driving force behind the murder. They also discarded the theory of a crime inspired by a television episode. Instead, their attention shifted towards workplace dynamics, especially after uncovering some level of animosity towards Angara among her coworkers.

Despite the known dislike from two female colleagues, no one believed it could escalate to murder. Angara was generally well-regarded: her dedication, cheerfulness, and humility – preferring her first name over her formal title "Doctor" – painted her as a respected and beloved figure. Her role as a senior chemist did not involve hiring or firing, further diminishing the likelihood of a severe workplace conflict.

The investigation then veered towards the possibility of an unplanned crime, perhaps sparked by a heated argument or Angara accidentally witnessing something incriminating. The theories involving the plant's technical issues, like discoloration and ozone problems, were ruled out, as was the malfunctioning of the displacement sensor.

Considering the physicality involved in the crime – lifting and replacing a heavy access panel and overpowering Angara, who was of considerable stature – the police initially leaned towards the likelihood of a male perpetrator. However, this was not a unanimous view; the county coroner suggested that a physically fit woman could also accomplish these tasks.

In a massive investigative effort, the Passaic County prosecutor's office assigned 13 detectives to the case. These dedicated officers invested over 4,000 hours in exhaustive interviews with all plant employees and collected DNA samples from those who were present on the day of the tragedy.

In the aftermath of Angara's tragic death, the atmosphere at the plant trans-formed dramatically. For safety and oversight, workers were mandated to operate in pairs, and police vigilance intensified, monitoring every movement within the plant with acute attention. This heightened scrutiny and the lingering unease of an unresolved murder among them began to fray the nerves of the employees, leading to heightened tensions and unease.

A striking example of this strained environment occurred a month following the incident, when two electricians, embroiled in a heated dispute over overtime, let their tempers flare. The argument escalated to the point where one electrician threatened to physically harm his colleague, a threat taken seriously enough for the police to intervene. The aggressor was subsequently suspended, illustrating the frayed nerves and volatile atmosphere within the plant.

Meanwhile, the investigators, delving deeper into the case, had narrowed their focus to a select group of eight men. General consensus among the employees suggested that Angara was well-liked, which further complicated the task of uncovering a motive for her murder. John Latoracca, the chief assistant prosecutor, conveyed his perplexity to The New York Times. He speculated that the murder could either be the result of a deeply concealed, powerful motive or an unplanned act, perhaps a confrontation that spiraled out of control.

A year into the investigation, the circle of suspicion had tightened even further, focusing on three primary suspects. Intriguingly, one of these suspects was the very coworker who had first noticed Angara's absence after his visit to the basement. James Wood, the chief homicide detective for the prosecutor's office, shared with The New York Post an anecdote about another suspect who seemed on the verge of confession, only to retract and cease cooperation upon obtaining legal counsel. Wood noted the absence of solid alibis among these suspects, all of whom had unimpeded access to the crime scene.

The investigators, piecing together the sequence of events and the nature of the crime, began to lean towards the theory of an impulsive, unplanned act. This perspective was encapsulated in Wood's candid remark to the media: "This killer isn't smart, just lucky."

The police, in their relentless pursuit of the truth, requested all three prime suspects to undergo polygraph tests, yielding a mixed bag of results: one suspect passed, another yielded inconclusive results, and the third outright refused to take the test. Despite re-interviewing these suspects following the polygraph tests, the investigators found themselves at a frustrating standstill, with no new revelations coming to light.

In a meticulous effort to leave no stone unturned, divers were dispatched to comb through the tanks, searching for any overlooked evidence. Simultaneously, federal and state environmental regulators were brought in to scrutinize the plant's records, hoping to unearth any anomalies that might have slipped past initial inspections. Despite these extensive efforts, the middle of 2006 arrived with the investigation mired in uncertainty, and the case tragically transitioned into a cold case. It stood as one of only two unsolved homicides out of the 30 reported in Passaic County that year.

In a move fueled by the persistence and hope of the Angara family, the state Attorney General's office was petitioned in 2007 to have the state police re-examine the case. Despite this renewed effort, the veil of mystery surrounding Angara's death remained unlifted, with no new developments emerging from this review.

The tragic incident had a lasting impact on the Passaic Valley Water Commission (PVWC). In the wake of Angara's death, the commission contracted for heightened security measures, including round-the-clock armed guards patrolling both inside and outside the plant. This response underscored the severity and the ripple effects of the crime within the organization.

Two years after the incident, in 2007, the Angara family took a significant legal step by filing a wrongful death lawsuit against the PVWC and some of its employees. They contended that the plant had a history of safety violations and accidents, citing the state's 55 citations against the plant. They argued that the commission had been negligent in addressing these safety concerns. The lawsuit's progress was slow, and after two years, it moved into mediation as ordered by a judge.

A decade after the killing, the case saw a glimmer of renewed attention when the Angara family, with the support of State Senator Joe Kyrillos, lobbied for another state-level review of the case. This advocacy led to a startling revelation by the police, suggesting a possible misjudgment regarding the three suspects initially believed to be involved. Chief Assistant Prosecutor Latoracca shared with The Star-Ledger that upon closer scrutiny of additional factors and re-interviews, the suspects, while initially appearing suspicious, were ultimately not believed to be directly responsible for Angara's death.

In their relentless pursuit to unravel the case, police investigators found themselves delving into the annals of unsolved mysteries, uncovering parallels with another haunting case from decades earlier. The detectives were struck by the eerie resemblance between Angara's case and an unsolved murder from 1968, which had remained a persistent enigma in their jurisdiction.

This earlier case involved 22-year-old Joan Freeman, a resident of what was then known as West Paterson. Her life met a tragic and violent end at the Hoffmann-La Roche plant complex, which spanned the border between Clifton in Passaic County and Nutley in neighboring Essex County. The grim discovery of Freeman's body on August 31, 1968, revealed a brutal attack: she had been ambushed from behind and struck multiple times on the head with a wooden mallet, followed by a vicious throat-slitting. The coroner's report was chilling, stating that any one of the inflicted wounds could have been fatal.

Passaic County authorities, tasked with investigating this heinous crime, noted its similarities to Angara's case: both involved minimal evidence at the crime scene and a limited number of potential suspects. Freeman, like Angara, had been working alone, handling overtime duties in a second-floor library of one of the 86 buildings on the pharmaceutical company's sprawling campus. The absence of fingerprints on the murder weapon and the missing knife used in the attack compounded the mystery. The security measures at the Hoffmann-La Roche campus mirrored those at the Totowa treatment plant, with stringent entry controls and a fenced perimeter, allowing only cleared individuals access.

Despite an exhaustive investigation into Freeman's personal life, detectives were unable to unearth a motive for the murder. The intensity of the investigation was profound, involving 16 investigators from the county prosecutor's office, state police, and Clifton police. They conducted interviews with 300 individuals who might have been on the campus that day, including administering lie detector tests. Yet, the breakthrough they desperately sought remained elusive. "Many times I went home and couldn't sleep," one of the detectives later reflected, lamenting the absence of a pivotal clue. The Freeman case, much like Angara's, remained an open, unsolved mystery, with detectives occasionally revisiting the files in hopes of new insights.

County Prosecutor Avigliano, recognizing the parallels between these two tragic cases, expressed his thoughts to The Star-Ledger: "The events are similar in nature. A woman was murdered in a secure facility." His office's detectives embarked on a thorough examination of the Freeman case. Their goal was twofold: to investigate any possible cross-employment between Hoffmann-La Roche and the PVWC, and to glean investigative insights from the Freeman case that might aid in solving Angara's murder.

Over a year had passed since the tragic and mysterious death of Angara, and the case, steeped in ambiguity and unanswered questions, took an unexpected turn in May 2006. Some investigators, exploring every conceivable angle, began to entertain a theory that veered sharply from the initial conclusion of homicide: the possibility that Angara's death might have been a tragic accident. This new line of inquiry led them to seek the expertise of Derrick Pounder, a Scottish forensic pathologist based at the University of Dundee. Renowned as one of the few specialists in the area of drownings, especially those occurring in cold water, Pounder's research offered a potentially pivotal perspective.

Pounder's studies had uncovered a phenomenon in a small fraction of cold-water drowning cases. In these rare instances, the victims exhibited bruising on the neck and petechiae in the eyeballs, symptoms traditionally associated with premortem strangulation. This revelation suggested the possibility that Angara's injuries, initially perceived as signs of a violent assault, could instead be the unfortunate result of a drowning accident.

However, there were significant limitations in applying Pounder's expertise directly to Angara's case. Notably, Pounder never had the opportunity to examine Angara's body, which had been cremated soon after her death in accordance with Hindu funerary traditions. Furthermore, he did not have access to the records from the autopsy. Despite these constraints, his insights offered a new dimension to the case.

County Prosecutor Avigliano acknowledged that the five medical examiners in Passaic County, who had examined Angara's body and autopsy records, were unanimous in their conclusion that her death was a homicide. Yet, this consensus was not shared by all members of the initial investigation team.

Adding to the evolving narrative of the case, the county's chief homicide detective, Wood, retired in 2006 after dedicating 18 months to the Angara investigation. By the time of the third anniversary of Angara's death, Wood's reflections, influenced in part by Pounder's research, had led him to a personal conclusion that diverged from the official stance. He began to lean towards the theory that Angara's death was accidental, a result of negligence rather than deliberate harm. Wood speculated that the access plate, central to the mystery of how Angara ended up in the tank, might have been removed prior to her entering the room.

The enigmatic circumstances surrounding Angara's death continued to fuel a myriad of theories and speculations. In a revealing conversation with The New York Post, an unnamed worker from the plant shed light on a potentially crucial aspect of the day Angara died. According to this worker, the state had mandated specific tests in response to a pinkish discoloration observed in the water. This testing protocol typically involved automated sample collection along the water path, but a supervisor at the plant, described as "very old school," insisted on a more traditional approach. This involved manually collecting water directly from the tank, a process necessitating the removal of the access plate.

Wood, reflecting on these details, formed a hypothesis that hinged on human error. He conjectured that someone, perhaps in a moment of negligence, forgot to replace the plate after completing the testing. When Angara later entered the dimly lit area, she might have tragically fallen into the unguarded opening. Wood speculated that the individual responsible for the plate, realizing the grave error, hastily replaced it, perhaps too aware of the liability they faced. "I don't think anyone will ever admit to taking that plate off or putting it back on because they know they're going to be held liable for it," Wood expressed in an interview with The Star-Ledger.

This theory of accidental death, however, met with skepticism, particularly from Angara's daughter. In 2015, she challenged this notion, emphasizing her mother's characteristic caution and vigilance. She found it implausible that her mother would have overlooked a large, ominous opening in the floor. This sentiment was echoed by other plant workers who claimed that they had never witnessed such panels being left open.

Angara's daughter pointed out that accepting the accident theory required disregarding numerous other facts, including the puzzling delay in her coworkers noticing her absence. The family remained troubled by the apparent oversight of her disappearance throughout the remainder of the workday.

At this juncture, the county prosecutor's office classified the case as "open but inactive." Latoracca, who had since transitioned to a private practice as a criminal defense attorney, acknowledged the perspectives that led Wood and other detectives to consider the possibility of an accident. Yet, he reiterated his confidence in the medical findings that suggested Angara's death was a result of intentional actions. This ongoing divergence of opinions and theories continued to cast a shadow of uncertainty and complexity over a case that had long eluded a definitive resolution.

Murder of Sarah Pryor

In the quaint town of Wayland, Massachusetts, a tragic mystery unfolded in the autumn of 1985. Sarah Pryor, a nine-year-old with a bright smile and a zest for life, became the central figure in a story that has haunted the community for decades. Born on January 13, 1976, to Andrew and Barbara Pryor, Sarah grew up in a nurturing family environment with her older siblings, Byron and Meg. The Pryors had recently moved from Pittsburgh, Pennsylvania, seeking a fresh start in the serene surroundings of Wayland.

Sarah, a charming girl with blonde hair, hazel eyes, and a distinctive gap between her front teeth, quickly adapted to her new home. She shared a special bond with her family, especially her beloved border collie, Katie. An outdoor enthusiast and a diligent student, Sarah embraced her new life with enthusiasm.

On a seemingly ordinary Wednesday, October 9, 1985, Sarah's routine was as usual. After school, she indulged in a bowl of Jell-O and relaxed with some television. Later, feeling the urge to step outside, she informed her father, Andrew, of her plan to take a stroll around the neighborhood. The conversation was light, with Andrew playfully nudging her to clean her dish, and Sarah assuring him she would do so upon her return. Rejecting her father's suggestion to take Katie along, citing the dog's slow pace, Sarah grabbed her Walkman and set out on her walk, a routine activity in her peaceful community.

However, this walk was different. When Andrew returned from taking Byron to football practice around 5:00 p.m., Sarah was nowhere to be found. The concern grew when Barbara arrived home at 5:50 p.m. to find Sarah still missing. What started as a simple neighborhood walk spiraled into a perplexing disappearance, leaving the Pryor family in a state of despair and uncertainty.

Years passed, and the mystery of Sarah's whereabouts remained unsolved. It wasn't until a decade later that a grim discovery was made. A man, walking his dog through a wooded area, stumbled upon a skull fragment. This fragment was later identified as belonging to Sarah, bringing a tragic closure to her disappearance. Despite suspicions and a primary suspect, no one has ever been held accountable for Sarah's abduction and murder.

In the wake of Sarah Pryor's mysterious disappearance, the town of Wayland, Massachusetts, transformed into a hive of desperate search activity. Police officers, accompanied by tracker dogs, led an extensive search operation, with over 2,000 volunteers joining in. They scoured fields and dense woods, fueled by hope and determination, but Sarah remained elusive. Even the deployment of an airplane equipped with sophisticated infrared detection technology failed to shed light on her whereabouts. The only clue that emerged was from witnesses who reported seeing Sarah walking along north Concord Road, a detail that only added to the growing anxiety.

The town rallied in an extraordinary display of unity and concern. Yellow ribbons, symbolizing hope and a warm welcome home, adorned mailboxes and trees, creating a poignant landscape of shared longing for Sarah's safe return. Missing posters with Sarah's image became a common sight throughout Wayland, a silent plea from a community shaken by the loss of one of its youngest members.

As time passed, various leads surfaced, igniting brief flares of hope, only to be extinguished by the cold reality of dead ends. One particularly chilling lead came from an anonymous source in Rhode Island, who claimed that Sarah's body lay in an abandoned well. This tip, like many others, led nowhere; the well was empty. Similarly, a man in West Virginia reported a sighting of Sarah, but it turned out to be a case of mistaken identity.

The case took a dramatic turn a few months later. Police detained a woman who confessed to participating in Sarah's kidnapping, along with two men. According to her account, they had taken Sarah to a housing project in Boston, where they tragically ended her life. This lead seemed promising enough to prompt the District Attorney to request media discretion, hoping to secure an arrest before the story broke. However, the media, sensing a sensational story, disregarded this plea and unleashed a frenzied report claiming Sarah had been brutally assaulted and her body discarded in Boston Harbor.

In a bizarre twist, one of the alleged accomplices mentioned by the woman was incarcerated in the same jail as the infamous crime boss James "Whitey" Bulger, housed at the Lawrence House of Correction. Bulger, who was secretly operating as a police informant at the time, was strategically placed in the same cell as the suspect. After intense interrogation sessions, Bulger reported back to the FBI that the suspect vehemently denied any involvement in Sarah's disappearance. Subsequently, the woman retracted her story, admitting that her motive was the reward money, not the truth.

As the years rolled by, the influx of leads dwindled, and the fervent energy that once drove the search for Sarah Pryor gradually waned. The case, shrouded in mystery and marred by false leads and dead ends, eventually went cold, leaving behind a lingering sense of unfinished justice and a community forever marked by the tragedy of a young girl's unexplained disappearance.

In 1987, two years after the perplexing disappearance of Sarah Pryor, an American journalist, Martin Yant, found himself in Germany, imbued with a sense of curiosity and exploration. While there, he made a deliberate visit to a monumental symbol of division and political tension – the Berlin Wall.

This wall, infamous for its representation of the Cold War divide, held an unexpected revelation for Yant. As he perused the Western side of the Wall, he was struck by the vibrant graffiti that adorned its surface. The presence of this artistic expression on such a historically significant structure was a revelation to him.

Among the myriad of colors and messages, one particular inscription, stark in its simplicity and emotional weight, caught Yant's attention. Painted in unassuming white letters, amidst the chaos of colors and words, was a heartfelt message dedicated to Sarah Pryor. The message, written in English, conveyed love and remembrance for the young girl who had vanished from Wayland, Massachusetts. It was a poignant reminder that Sarah's story had resonated far beyond her hometown, touching hearts across the ocean.

This discovery intrigued Yant, prompting him to contact authorities in Wayland. However, he learned that they were already aware of this distant tribute to Sarah. The identity of the person who had taken the time to inscribe Sarah's memory on the Berlin Wall remained a mystery. This graffiti stood as a silent sentinel until the fall of the Berlin Wall in late 1989, a symbol of the global reach of a local tragedy.

Eight years later, in 1995, the mystery of Sarah's disappearance took a grim turn. A man, out walking his dog near the Weston border, stumbled upon a fragment of a skull in a wooded area. The discovery prompted an investigation, and the remains were handed over to the state medical examiner. However, the medical examiner could not make a definitive identification, leaving the case shrouded in uncertainty.

In 1997, a forensic anthropologist examined the skull fragment and concluded that it belonged to a child around Sarah's age. The fragment, according to the anthropologist's estimation, had been lying in the woods for a period ranging between three to fifteen years. This finding aligned disturbingly with the timeline of Sarah's disappearance.

The case took a significant turn when the Middlesex County District Attorney's office sought the expertise of the Armed Forces Institute of Pathology (AFIP). While the AFIP typically handled military cases, they made an exception for this one. Their scientists managed to extract several strands of nuclear DNA from the fragment. However, without a direct sample from Sarah's body, a definitive match remained elusive. The breakthrough came with the extraction of mitochondrial DNA, which is passed from mother to child. The DA's office then requested blood samples from Barbara Pryor and her daughter, Meg, to compare with the DNA from the skull fragment.

The samples were sent to a lab on December 22, 1997. The subsequent analysis revealed a match – the skull fragment belonged to Sarah Pryor. This revelation brought a somber closure to the long-standing mystery of Sarah's fate.

On January 13, 1998, which would have been Sarah's 22nd birthday, the community came together to bid a final farewell to the girl whose life was tragically cut short. Around 1,000 people gathered to attend Sarah's funeral, a testament to the profound impact her story had on the hearts of many. This solemn occasion marked the end of a long and painful journey for Sarah's family and the community, as they finally laid to rest a beloved daughter, sister, and friend, whose memory had traversed continents and touched countless lives.

As the investigation into Sarah Pryor's disappearance unfolded, the focus eventually shifted to potential suspects, revealing a disturbing trail of criminal activity that spanned years and states. Two individuals, in particular, emerged as suspects, one soon after Sarah's disappearance and another almost a decade and a half later, each with a chilling history of violence.

The first suspect, John Whirty, had a particularly alarming past. Back in 1966, when he was just 21 years old, Whirty was charged with assaulting a 12-year-old girl in Sherborn, Massachusetts. However, evading the clutches of the law, he fled to Texas before his trial could commence. In March 1967, Whirty's criminal tendencies escalated horrifically. He lured 15-year-old Rose Marie Martin to a secluded area near White Rock Lake in Dallas, where he committed a heinous crime – raping and strangling her. Convicted for this brutal act, Whirty was sentenced to life in prison, only to be released on parole in 1984, a decision that would have dire consequences.

Around two months before Sarah Pryor vanished, another young girl, Cathy Malcolmson, 17, went missing under mysterious circumstances. Cathy had left her home in Stow, Massachusetts, on her bicycle to pick up her paycheck from the IGA supermarket in Hudson, but she never reached her destination. Initially thought to be a runaway, the case took a sinister turn in 1987 when her bicycle was discovered in a wooded area near the Stowe border. Cathy's body, however, has never been found, adding another layer of tragedy to the story.

The cases of Cathy and Sarah began to draw parallels in the eyes of the authorities, who suspected a connection. This theory gained traction a month after Sarah's disappearance, when Whirty made a bold and dangerous move in Newton, Massachusetts. He attempted to abduct a young-looking 20-year-old woman at knifepoint. The woman's narrow escape and the quick thinking of a cab driver, who noted Whirty's license plate, led to his identification as the assailant.

Further investigation into Whirty's car revealed a disturbing detail: the interior door handle on the passenger side was conspicuously missing. This discovery became a critical piece of evidence, suggesting a premeditated intent to prevent escape. The coverage of Whirty's arrest by local media prompted two witnesses to step forward, claiming they had seen him on the bike path at the time Sarah Pryor was known to be walking there.

Whirty's actions in Massachusetts constituted a violation of his parole for the murder of Rose Marie Martin. After serving a five-year sentence for the attempted abduction in Newton, authorities transferred him back to Texas to face the consequences of violating his parole. He is currently serving a life sentence for Rose's murder, a grim reminder of the potential danger he posed to Sarah and Cathy, and perhaps others.

In December 1999, a harrowing revelation emerged in the ongoing mystery of Sarah Pryor's disappearance. Hadden Clark, a convicted murderer and suspected serial killer serving time in Maryland, confided to a cellmate a chilling confession. He claimed that during a visit to his father's house near Wayland in 1985, he had encountered and killed a young girl named Sarah. Clark's account was particularly gruesome: he alleged to have consumed part of her remains before burying her in Wellfleet. The specific details he provided about the girl and the circumstances of her disappearance bore a disturbing resemblance to Sarah Pryor's case.

In an attempt to verify Clark's confession, authorities brought him to the specified property in Wellfleet, accompanied by a recovery dog, in search of any remains. However, this effort was overshadowed by the fact that parts of Sarah's remains had already been discovered near Weston, leaving the truth of Clark's claim in doubt. Clark is currently serving two consecutive 30-year sentences at the Eastern Correctional Institution in Maryland for two unrelated but equally heinous murders - that of six-year-old Michelle Dorr in 1986, and 23-year-old Laura Houghteling in 1992.

Despite these alarming confessions and the shadow of suspicion cast over figures like John Whirty and Hadden Clark, the case of Sarah Pryor's abduction and murder remains unsolved. No charges have been brought against either man in connection with Sarah's case.

The tragic loss of Sarah had far-reaching effects beyond the investigation. It deeply impacted the Pryor family, particularly her parents, Andrew and Barbara Pryor. The strain of the tragedy, compounded by Andrew's struggles with alcohol, took a heavy toll on their marriage. The couple, grappling with the immense weight of their loss, separated three years after Sarah's disappearance and eventually divorced around 1990.

In a touching tribute to Sarah, a memorial was erected in 1996 at Hanna Williams Park in Wayland. The sculptor, Nancy Schön, was approached by Sarah's mother, who shared heartwarming memories of her daughter, particularly her love for sledding with her Border Collie, Katie. Inspired by these stories, Schön created "Empty Sled and Dog," a sculpture that captures the essence of Sarah's spirit and the joy she found in simple childhood pleasures. This living, interactive memorial stands not just as a reminder of Sarah, but as a celebration of her life and the exuberance of all children.

Tragedy struck the Pryor family again in July 2014 when Andrew Pryor was involved in a devastating car accident, leaving him paralyzed from the chest down. He succumbed to his injuries on August 3, 2014, adding another layer of sorrow to the family's story.

The investigation into the abduction and murder of Sarah Pryor continues, a testament to the enduring hope for resolution and justice in a case that has left an indelible mark on the community and all who have been touched by the story of a young girl whose life was tragically cut short.

Murder of Robert Wone

Robert Wone's story begins on June 1, 1971, in the bustling borough of Brooklyn, New York. He was the firstborn son to William and Aimee Wone, marking the arrival of a fourth-generation Chinese American in a family whose roots traced back to the great-grandparents who bravely immigrated from China in the 1930s. The Wone family, deeply rooted in New York's rich cultural tapestry, nurtured Robert in an environment filled with love and tradition.

From an early age, Robert's character shone brightly. He was the epitome of kindness and competence, a beacon of warmth in his community. His childhood was marked by an effortless ability to forge friendships and a natural inclination towards altruism. Stories of his generosity became the stuff of local legend; he was the student who, under the veil of night, would diligently clean school statues, removing the unsightly bird droppings. He was also the anonymous benefactor who dropped coins into expired parking meters, saving countless strangers from unwelcome tickets. Robert's deeds, big and small, were driven not by the desire for recognition but by a pure heart.

Describing Robert as merely 'promising' would be a disservice to his extraordinary potential. His academic journey took him to the esteemed College of William and Mary in Virginia, where his brilliance and dedication did not go unnoticed. He served as an aide to the university's President, seamlessly integrating into a circle of friends who shared his ambition and drive. It was here that Robert's path crossed with Joseph Price, a like-minded individual destined for a successful career in law. Their bond solidified as they revitalized a campus secret society, the 13 Club, dedicated to clandestine acts of kindness, further cementing their shared values.

Robert's academic pursuits continued to soar as he obtained a law degree from the University of Pennsylvania in 1999. His legal acumen led him to the prestigious corridors of Covington & Burling, where he quickly became a respected figure in the Asian-American legal community. His professional trajectory was a testament to his hard work and intelligence.

In January 2002, at a legal conference, fate introduced Robert to Katherine Yu. Kathy, as she was affectionately known, was a daughter of Korean immigrants and had grown up in Chicago. She was not only Robert's equal in terms of her impressive academic credentials but also shared his passion for law. Their connection was instant and profound, leading to a long-term relationship that swiftly evolved into a deep commitment. Robert's proposal came within a year, and by 2003, they celebrated their union in a wedding that marked the beginning of a beautiful, loving marriage.

By 2006, Robert and Kathy had built a life that many dream of – fulfilling careers, a supportive circle of friends, and a future that shone with promise. However, life's unpredictable nature meant that their journey together would not follow the happy path they had envisioned.

In the early summer of 2006, Robert Wone found himself at a crossroads, yearning for more than just professional success. He was thriving as a lawyer at Covington & Burling in Washington D.C., but his heart was calling him to serve the community in a more meaningful way. He shared with his wife, Kathy, his aspiration to join Radio Free Asia, a non-profit news organization dedicated to providing unfiltered news to communities in Asia that lacked access to uncensored media.

This career shift would likely mean a significant cut in Robert's income, but Kathy fully supported his decision. She recognized the importance of his personal fulfillment and believed in his vision. Her stable position at a healthcare consulting firm reassured them that they could manage financially.

Robert embarked on the interview journey with determination and soon secured the position at Radio Free Asia. By early August, he was immersing himself in this new, exciting role. On August 2nd, Robert had plans to attend a legal seminar in the evening in Washington D.C., an event he was keenly looking forward to. Following the seminar, he intended to visit the Radio Free Asia offices to meet with the second-shift staff, a gesture underscoring his commitment to his new role.

After discussing it with Kathy, they concluded that staying overnight in D.C. would be more practical than the cumbersome journey back to their Oakton, Virginia condo using public transport. Coincidentally, Robert's college friend, Joseph Price, whom Kathy also knew and trusted, lived conveniently near Dupont Circle, offering an ideal place for Robert to stay. This arrangement seemed like the perfect solution, aligning neatly with Robert's plans for the evening.

Joe Price and Robert Wone's friendship began during their college years at William and Mary. After graduating in 2003, Joe pursued his law degree at the University of Virginia. His involvement in the LGBTQ+ community was significant, and upon completing his studies at UVa, he took on the role of president of the Gay and Lesbian Alumni Association. By 2006, Joe's career had flourished, and he had become a partner at Arent Fox, a prestigious national law firm with offices in Washington DC.

Alongside his professional achievements, Joe's personal life was equally fulfilling. He was in a long-standing relationship with Victor Zaborsky, a Senior Marketing Manager for Milk PEP, the organization behind the iconic "Got Milk?" campaigns. The couple, actively engaged in the gay community, co-parented two sons with a lesbian couple. In 2004, they expanded their family unit to include Dylan Ward, a Georgetown graduate with a varied career path. The trio purchased a luxurious $1.2 million townhome near Dupont Circle and lived together in a polyamorous relationship, with Joe often regarded as the central figure in their dynamic.

This unconventional family hosted Robert Wone's 30th birthday party in 2004, demonstrating the depth of their friendship with both Robert and his wife Kathy. Joe and Victor had even celebrated with the Wones at their wedding in 2003. So, when Robert suggested staying at Price's townhome on August 2, 2006, Kathy had no reservations about it, trusting in the long-standing bond between their families.

August 2nd began as a typical day for Kathy and Robert Wone. They started with a morning gym session near their Oakton home, followed by a shared metro ride into Washington DC. The couple's routine included a parting kiss before diverging to their respective workplaces, followed by a customary email to each other confirming their safe arrival—a small yet significant daily ritual.

Robert's day proceeded with his usual work responsibilities, culminating in a continuing education legal seminar he attended after office hours. This event concluded around 9:30 pm, and he called Kathy from a cab on his way back to the Radio Free Asia office, where he planned to meet the night staff. He informed her that afterwards, he would catch a cab to Joe Price's residence and then retire for the night. This conversation would tragically be the last time Kathy heard her husband's voice.

The calm of the night was shattered at 12:06 am when Kathy received a distressing call from Joe Price. His words were chilling: "Kathy, I can't believe I'm calling you about this. Go over to George Washington Hospital. Robert has been stabbed in the back." This information, later sourced to a Washingtonian article, sent Kathy into a state of shock.

She immediately reached out to her in-laws, who had recently relocated to the area from Brooklyn, New York to be closer to the couple. Robert's younger brother, also in town for a visit, joined the family as they hurried to George Washington Hospital, expecting to find Robert fighting for his life. However, upon arrival, they were met with the devastating news that Robert had already passed away. Compounding their grief was the discovery that the wounds inflicted were to his chest and stomach, contrary to what Joe Price had initially informed Kathy. At the moment, Kathy may not have dwelled on this inconsistency, but it would later emerge as the first of many discrepancies in a complex and bewildering murder investigation that would envelop the tragic demise of her husband.

On the evening of August 2, 2006, at 11:49 pm, a 911 call was placed to a dispatcher in Washington DC from a distraught Victor Zaborsky at 1509 Swann Street, N.W. His voice, laced with panic and tears, conveyed the urgency of needing an ambulance. He explained that an intruder had apparently entered their home and stabbed a friend who was staying over.

The dispatcher, seeking to understand the situation, inquired if someone was bleeding. Victor, barely containing his distress, confirmed that their friend was bleeding from his stomach. As the dispatcher asked about the friend's breathing, Victor admitted his uncertainty. He explained that his partner, Joe Price, was with the injured friend on the second floor, the site of the stabbing, while he had retreated upstairs to call for help.

The dispatcher's questions turned to the identity of the assailant, but Victor insisted they had no idea who was responsible. She advised him to apply pressure to the wound with a towel, giving detailed instructions: use a towel, and when it's soaked with blood, place another one on top without removing the first. In the background of the call, Victor's voice could be heard urging someone to apply pressure to the wound.

Victor's description of the injuries—a wound to the stomach and possibly the heart—signaled to the dispatcher a scenario of significant blood loss. Such injuries typically result in a substantial amount of blood, yet the unfolding events of this case were far from typical.

When paramedics arrived minutes later, they encountered a scene that was unnervingly abnormal, one of them later recalling how it made "the hair on the back of [his] neck stand up."

The 911 operator instructed Victor to open the door for the paramedics. As he moved downstairs, he offered unsolicited information, suggesting the assailant might have fled the house with one of their knives. Yet again, when asked if he knew who committed the act, Victor's response was a firm denial of any knowledge.

Five minutes after Victor Zaborsky's frantic 911 call at 11:49 pm, paramedics arrived at the Swann Street residence. They found Victor on the porch, donned in a white terry cloth bathrobe, still on the phone, pleading for help for the stabbing victim on the second floor, before breaking into uncontrollable sobs.

With a combined experience of 25 years, the paramedics were seasoned in emergency response. Typically, stabbing scenes were chaotic, with occupants in distress and frantically guiding them to the victim. This scene, however, was strikingly different: apart from Victor's distress on the porch, the other inhabitants seemed eerily calm and composed.

As they ascended the stairs, they came across Dylan Ward, emerging from a second-floor bathroom, freshly showered and wearing a robe. Despite their inquiries, he offered no response, walking past them into a bedroom and shutting the door.

In the guest room, the paramedics found 32-year-old Robert Wone on a neatly made pull-out sofa bed. Contrary to their instructions, no one was applying pressure to his stab wounds. Joseph Price, the homeowner, was seated on the bed in his underwear, back to the door, nonchalantly stating he had heard a scream.

The paramedics found Price's demeanor unsettling, prompting them to check his hands for weapons and position themselves strategically to both tend to Wone and keep an eye on Price.

Robert lay with his head on a pillow, his hands by his sides, still wearing his mouthguard, in a William and Mary T-shirt. He had three stab wounds on his torso, visible through the shirt. The paramedics noted the severity of the heart wound, large enough to fit a finger.

A knife with a faint trace of blood, presumed to be the murder weapon, lay on the bedside table.

Robert had no pulse, indicating he had been deceased for some time. An EKG confirmed a flat line - no heart activity. He was transported to the hospital, where he was officially pronounced dead at 12:25 am.

Robert Wone had arrived at the home shared by Joseph Price, Victor Zaborsky, and Dylan Ward at 10:30 pm that night. By 12:25 am on August 3rd, he was dead. The circumstances of his death, the perplexing state of the crime scene, and the behavior of the last people to see him alive raised a multitude of questions for the police. As they began their investigation, they focused on gathering information from the three individuals who had last seen Robert Wone alive.

Upon arriving at the scene, the Metropolitan Police Department immediately observed the strikingly orderly state of the guest room where Robert Wone's body was found. Contrary to expectations of a violent intrusion, there was no apparent disarray: Robert's work clothes were neatly folded at the foot of the bed, and his personal items, including a wallet, Blackberry, and expensive watch, lay untouched on a nearby table. The lack of disruption suggested that robbery was unlikely the motive.

The scene suggested an absence of physical struggle. The sole indentation on Robert's pillow indicated he hadn't moved during the attack, an unusual detail given the severity of his injuries.

Surprisingly, Robert's body bore minimal blood, an anomaly for someone with multiple stab wounds. There was only a faint smear of blood on his abdomen, seemingly wiped across his skin intentionally.

Equally puzzling was the near absence of blood on the bed. Aside from two small stains beneath his body, the bed was remarkably clean. The sheet was meticulously folded, and Robert appeared almost pristine, as if he had been cleaned, redressed, and placed on the bed.

The investigators found a knife on the bedside table, sourced from a kitchen knife block, but doubted it was the murder weapon. Its blade was longer than the entry wounds on Robert's chest, and it lacked blood on the cutting edge and any cotton fibers from his T-shirt. A missing knife from a cutlery set in Dylan Ward's room, matching the wounds' depth, raised further suspicions, but this knife was never found.

A white cotton towel near the bed, alleged by the three men to have been used to stem Robert's bleeding, presented another incongruity. The bloodstains on it were minimal and inconsistent with what would be expected from such a use. Instead, they resembled stains from wiping blood off a knife.

The forensic evidence starkly contradicted the men's accounts, casting doubt on their explanations.

Police took Ward, Price, and Zaborsky to the station for separate interviews, but their stories were uniformly aligned, adding to the mystery and complexity of the case.

On the night of his tragic demise, Robert Wone arrived at the residence shared by Joseph Price, Victor Zaborsky, and Dylan Ward around 10:30 pm, traveling by taxi. At that time, Victor Zaborsky had just returned from a business trip and was in bed, watching "Project Runway" upstairs.

According to Price and Ward, they briefly joined Wone in the kitchen for water and conversation before showing him to the guest room. Price then retired to the third-floor master bedroom he shared with Zaborsky, while Ward claimed to have gone to his own room on the second floor. Ward recalled reading for a short while, taking a sleeping pill, and then going to bed. He mentioned hearing Wone showering in the hallway bathroom, followed by the sound of the guest room door closing and latching.

Later, Price and Zaborsky reported being awakened by the sound of their house alarm, which chimed when exterior doors were opened. They initially dismissed it, assuming it was Sarah, their fourth roommate, coming home. However, they were soon alerted by a series of low grunts or screams. Rushing down to the second floor, they found Wone in his guest room, lying on the bed with stab wounds, and the room door slightly open.

They reported no subsequent door chimes or sounds of someone descending the stairs.

Price instructed Zaborsky to call 911 from upstairs while he attempted to stem Wone's bleeding. Price claimed to have found the presumed murder weapon on Wone's stomach, which he then moved to a side table. He noted to the police that his DNA might be on the knife due to this action, but speculated that the "real killer" might have worn gloves, leaving no DNA trace.

Price mentioned that he did not see Ward until after Zaborsky had gone to call 911. Zaborsky supported this account, stating that Ward was not present when they initially discovered Robert but emerged from his bedroom by the time Zaborsky returned downstairs on the phone with 911.

The three men concurred in their belief that an intruder was responsible for Wone's murder, speculating that the assailant might have scaled the security fence and entered through the back door.

Investigators were skeptical about the intruder theory proposed by Price, Zaborsky, and Ward. Their doubts were fueled by the lack of disturbance on the fence surrounding the property. An examination revealed untouched cobwebs and dust, suggesting no recent activity. Additionally, the house was filled with valuable electronics that remained untouched, casting further doubt on the notion of a break-in.

The supposed intruder's path also raised questions. To reach Wone in the guest room, the intruder would have had to bypass Dylan Ward's room, suggesting a specific target. This level of knowledge about Wone's presence indicated that only a few people, namely Kathy Wone, Price, Zaborsky, and Ward, were aware of his stay.

The police employed cadaver dogs skilled in detecting blood and decomposition. Apart from the minimal blood found on Wone's bed, the only other traces discovered were in the dryer lint trap near Dylan Ward's room and near an outside drain on the patio. This finding led to speculation that someone might have cleaned blood off themselves on the patio and then dried their clothes on the second floor.

According to official documents, the investigators noted the close relationship among Price, Zaborsky, and Ward, suggesting a strong motive to protect each other's interests.

The trio provided details about their relationship and living arrangements at 1509 Swann Street. Zaborsky informed the investigators that he and Price had been in a long-term committed relationship and had included Dylan in their relationship about four years prior. Dylan was sexually involved with Price but not with Zaborsky.

During their search, police found various BDSM-related items in Dylan's room, including shackles, gags, restraints, and an array of sex toys. The men explained that Dylan and Joe were engaged in a dominant/submissive sexual dynamic, with Dylan as the dominant partner.

Also discovered was a device often termed a "milking machine," designed for forced male ejaculation. This piece of evidence gained significance in light of the autopsy results of Robert Wone's body.

The autopsy of Robert Wone, conducted on August 3 by Dr. Lois Goslinoski, revealed several critical findings. She identified three symmetrical stab wounds on Robert's torso, each made with a blade approximately 4 ½ inches long, and 4 to 5 inches deep. This evidence contradicted the knife found at the scene, suggesting it was not the murder weapon.

Moreover, Dr. Goslinoski observed a broken blood vessel in Robert's eye, a sign of possible smothering. She also noted needle marks on his neck, chest, right foot, and left hand, all inflicted before his death. Despite running a standard drug scan that returned negative, she did not test for paralytic agents, and unfortunately, no blood samples were preserved before Robert's burial for further examination.

Remarkably, there were no defensive wounds on Robert's body, indicating no struggle during the attack. This lack of resistance suggested he may have been immobilized during the assault.

Dr. Goslinoski conducted a rape kit, finding semen in various bodily cavities. However, DNA analysis revealed that all the semen belonged to Robert Wone himself.

Piecing together Dr. Goslinoski's findings and the evidence from the crime scene, police hypothesized that Robert had been attacked, possibly immobilized with a paralytic agent, sexually assaulted, and then fatally stabbed on the night of August 2.

Adding to the complexity of the case, a timeline discrepancy emerged. A neighbor reported hearing a scream from the house during the nightly news, which aired between 11 and 11:30 pm. Yet, Victor Zaborsky's 911 call was not made until 11:49 pm, indicating a gap of at least 19 minutes between the discovery of the body and the emergency call.

Despite these revelations, the police faced a significant challenge: they lacked definitive evidence to identify the perpetrator. Meanwhile, Price, Zaborsky, and Ward ceased cooperation with the investigation, having retained attorneys following their initial questioning by the police.

The day after Robert Wone's tragic murder, Joseph Price, Victor Zaborsky, and Dylan Ward visited Kathy Wone to offer condolences. They mourned together, with Kathy initially unaware of the inconsistencies in their stories. Joe Price even took a significant role in Robert's funeral, serving as a pallbearer. However, as suspicions about the truthfulness of the trio's accounts emerged, a distance grew between them and Kathy.

Two weeks after the murder, the police publicly expressed their belief that the crime scene had been tampered with. They indicated, as reported in Legal Times, that the area around Robert's body had been cleaned, suggesting deliberate alteration of the crime scene.

By the first anniversary of the murder, the mystery remained unsolved, with police still unable to identify the perpetrator or fully understand the crime. Kathy Wone, accompanied by her attorney Eric Holder, who had worked with Robert at his previous law firm and later became Attorney General under President Barack Obama, held a press conference. They aimed to reinvigorate the stalled investigation.

At this press conference, Holder directly addressed Price, Ward, and Zaborsky.

He challenged them to reflect deeply on whether they had provided all relevant information to the police. He emphasized the moral responsibility they held if they truly cared about Robert, his family, and Kathy, urging them to come forward with any additional information they might possess. This heartfelt appeal underscored the ongoing quest for truth and justice in the perplexing case of Robert Wone's death.

Despite the impassioned plea made during the press conference, the speech did not have the desired effect of compelling Joseph Price, Victor Zaborsky, and Dylan Ward to divulge more information. In November 2008, frustrated by the lack of progress, DC prosecutors took decisive action. They charged all three men with obstruction of justice, beginning with Dylan Ward, followed by Price and Zaborsky.

Only six days after these charges, Kathy Wone initiated a $20 million civil lawsuit. She accused the trio of failing to assist her husband after he was stabbed and alleged that they spent the final moments of Robert's life concealing a heinous crime.

The criminal trial eventually commenced in the summer of 2010. Despite the mounting suspicious circumstantial evidence, Judge Lynn Leibovitz expressed her doubts about their guilt in the obstruction of justice charges. In her view, although it seemed evident that Ward, Price, and Zaborsky were aware of the identity of Robert's killer, she could not convict them based on the standard of 'beyond a reasonable doubt.' Consequently, she acquitted them of the charges.

In August 2011, the civil suit brought by Kathy Wone was settled out of court for an undisclosed sum. Speaking to a reporter from the Washington Post, Kathy conveyed her decision to put the past behind her. She expressed a desire to focus on positive aspects of life for the next four decades, leaving the burden of their secrets to Price, Ward, and Zaborsky. She stated her choice to move forward, contrasting it with their choice to live with the secrets they kept.

While the exact circumstances of Robert Wone's murder remain a mystery, the police have formed suspicions, albeit without concrete evidence to support them.

One avenue of suspicion involves Joseph Price's brother, Michael Price, known for his troubled history. Notably, three months after Robert's murder, Joseph Price's townhome was burglarized, and Michael was implicated in the crime. Although the charges were eventually dropped, the police delved into Michael's whereabouts on the night of the murder. They discovered he had missed a scheduled class at Montgomery College on the evening of August 2, 2006. Given Joseph Price's history of helping his brother out of difficult situations, it's plausible that if Michael had been involved in the murder, Joseph might have altered the crime scene to protect him. However, this remains speculative, as no definitive evidence supports this theory.

Another possibility is that some combination of events, possibly involving the other three men in the house that night - Joseph Price, Victor Zaborsky, and Dylan Ward - led to the tragedy. The behavior of these three men on the night of the murder, along with the peculiarities of the crime scene, raises significant questions. Their actions and the proximity of the crime to their sleeping quarters cast doubt on their claims of ignorance regarding the events of that night.

Regrettably, whatever knowledge these three men might possess about the incident seems to be a secret they are determined to keep. The reality is that unless Price, Zaborsky, and Ward choose to come forward with the truth, the details of what transpired in their townhouse on that fateful night may never be known. The tragic loss of Robert Wone, a person remembered for his kindness and generosity, remains an unresolved injustice.

It's a situation filled with frustration and sorrow. One can only hope that, eventually, the conscience of those who hold the answers will compel them to speak, bringing closure to this heartbreaking story. Until then, the case of Robert Wone remains an unsolved and haunting mystery.

2006 Ulvila Homicide

On the early morning of December 1st, 2006, a chilling emergency call was made at precisely 2:43 am. The frantic voice on the other end belonged to Anneli Orvokki Auer, born on March 19th, 1965. In a state of sheer panic, she screamed, "There's someone here, a killer, come quickly!" Auer relayed a horrifying scene: a mysterious intruder had broken into her home and violently attacked her husband, 51-year-old Jukka S. Lahti (born in 1955). She claimed that she, too, had been injured in the onslaught.

The household was not just a scene of violence but also a home to their four young children, aged 2, 4, 7, and 9, at the time of this dreadful incident. During the chaos, at least two of the eldest children were awoken, witnessing parts of this horrifying event. The emergency call, a desperate plea for help, spanned an intense four minutes, during which Auer was away from the phone for a heart-stopping 59 seconds.

Responding with urgency, the first officers arrived at the Auer residence approximately three minutes after the distress call. What they encountered was a gruesome scene: Lahti lay in a pool of blood on the bedroom floor. Paramedics rushed to the site shortly after, but their efforts were in vain; they pronounced Lahti dead at the scene. This tragic event left more questions than answers, painting a picture of a peaceful family night turned into a horrifying nightmare.

In a detailed account of that fateful night, Anneli Orvokki Auer painted a vivid and terrifying picture of the events leading to her husband's murder. The evening began routinely, with Jukka S. Lahti returning home from a work trip around 11 pm. After some time spent unwinding, the couple retired to bed at midnight, expecting a peaceful night's sleep. However, at approximately 2:40 am, their tranquility was shattered by a disturbing commotion—a strange man was breaking into their bedroom through the window. Auer described this harrowing moment in detail, noting that the process of the window breaking took about a minute.

In the pitch darkness of their room, the intruder, described as wearing a black hoodie and possibly a balaclava, leapt through the broken window and immediately launched an attack on Lahti. In a desperate attempt to defend himself, Lahti grabbed two pieces of firewood. Auer, in her bid to assist her husband, faced the assailant's wrath. The attacker, whom she estimated to be about 180 cm tall, struck her in the chest with a knife. Realizing the gravity of the situation, Auer recognized the intruder as a murderer and made a split-second decision to flee for help.

In a state of panic, Auer opened the front door and screamed for her children to evacuate the house, but her calls went unheard. She then rushed to the kitchen to make an emergency call using the landline. Meanwhile, the eldest child, awakened by the noise, had a chilling encounter. Upon Auer's request, the child came to the phone to hold the line while Auer returned to the bedroom to attempt another rescue.

Back in the bedroom, Auer faced the intruder once more, but was attacked twice, forcing her to flee the room again. During this terrifying ordeal, she was away from the phone for a critical 59 seconds. Upon her return, she continued the call for help. In a shocking twist, the eldest child, while waiting on the phone, witnessed a figure clad in dark clothing making an escape through the window. The child's glimpse into the bedroom revealed a horrifying sight: their father, Lahti, lying on the floor covered in blood.

The prosecutor's version of the events on that tragic night presents a starkly different narrative from Anneli Orvokki Auer's account, suggesting a deeply troubled relationship culminating in a violent confrontation. According to the prosecutor, when Jukka S. Lahti returned from his work trip around 11 pm, tensions between the couple quickly escalated into a heated argument. This was not just a spontaneous quarrel; the prosecution painted a picture of a relationship marred by fundamental differences in values and morals, even to the point where the couple had contemplated divorce.

The argument spiraled out of control, turning physically violent. Objects were thrown in a fit of rage, and soon, firewood and knives were wielded as weapons in a chaotic domestic battle. In a critical turn of events, Lahti allegedly struck Auer with a knife, wounding her on the side. However, the tables turned when Auer managed to gain control of the knife. In a moment of heightened aggression, she struck Lahti, causing him to lose consciousness. Believing she had fatally wounded him, Auer reportedly embarked on a calculated and cold-blooded plan to cover up her actions.

The prosecution accused Auer of meticulously staging the crime scene to mislead investigators into thinking an outsider had committed the murder. This staging allegedly involved breaking the bedroom window and creating bloody footprints using Lahti's shoes. In a further twist, as Auer was on the phone with the public-safety answering point, Lahti purportedly regained consciousness and began to shout. Seizing this moment, Auer allegedly asked her eldest child to hold the phone line while she returned to the bedroom. There, according to the prosecutor, she delivered two fatal blows to Lahti's head, resulting in his immediate death.

The prosecution also presented an alternative theory: Lahti might have been dead even before Auer made the emergency call. The noises heard in the background of the call, they suggested, could have come from a recording Auer had prepared earlier to support her fabricated story.

After returning to the phone, Auer's eldest child looked into the bedroom and thought they saw an outsider fleeing the scene, a detail that played into Auer's alleged ruse. The prosecution also noted that Auer had hidden the murder weapon and her blood-stained clothes so effectively that the police were unable to locate them.

The investigation into the murder of Jukka S. Lahti was a complex and intricate affair, marked by a series of revelations and perplexing findings. The first officers on the scene arrived just nine minutes after the emergency call was initiated. They were immediately confronted with a grisly sight: Lahti's lifeless body lay on the floor, surrounded by blood and broken glass. Near him, a Fiskars knife and a piece of bloody firewood were found. Strikingly, the actual weapon used for the killing—a heavy, blunt object—remained elusive, as it was never found at the crime scene or elsewhere.

In the bedroom, the scene was equally harrowing. Another piece of firewood was discovered on the blood-stained bed. DNA analysis revealed traces belonging to both Lahti and an unidentified individual, adding a layer of mystery to the investigation. Officers also recovered a black glove from the bed, a potential clue in piecing together the events of that night. Bloodied footprints led from the floor to the outside terrace, and bloody glove prints were found on the window frame. Crime scene investigator Matti Mäkinen initially asserted that the window had been broken from the outside. However, this assessment was later contradicted by the Pori police, who suggested that the breakage occurred from the inside, citing the distribution of glass shards both inside the room and on the terrace.

The investigative team faced another puzzle: numerous brown synthetic fibers were found at various locations within the crime scene, including the window frame, the terrace, and on Lahti himself. Yet, the origin of these fibers remained a mystery, as none were found on the red shirt worn by Auer.

Approximately an hour and a half after the murder, police dogs were brought to the scene in an attempt to track the murderer's scent. However, this effort was hampered by the extensive movement of officers in and around the house, contaminating potential scent trails. A trace was picked up in the neighbor's yard, but who had left it remained unknown. Intriguingly, the dogs found no connection between Auer and the knife alleged to have been used in the murder.

Initially, the focus of the investigation was on the possibility of personal vengeance linked to Lahti's professional life. He was a manager at Luvata, a copper factory, which had recently laid off 400 employees. This detail led investigators to speculate that the murder could be a carefully planned act of retribution. The nature of the murder and the calculated manner in which the assailant operated suggested to the police that the murderer might have psychopathic tendencies. Adding to this theory, Lahti had reportedly received threats prior to his murder, although he never specified any details about them.

In a bid to gather more information, Inspector Juha Joutsenlahti made a public appeal for help in locating a red Volvo passenger car. This vehicle had been spotted in the neighborhood on the night of the murder and also a week prior, raising suspicions about its connection to the crime. The police investigation revealed that sounds presumed to be made by an outsider were recorded in the emergency call, and they had also obtained DNA evidence from the crime scene, specifically from the bed, which they believed belonged to the killer. This led to one of Finland's most extensive DNA sample collections, with over 700 samples taken. However, this massive effort did not yield any significant breakthroughs in the case.

In a surprising twist in 2013, it was revealed that the unknown DNA found at the crime scene, which had long been believed to be that of the killer, actually belonged to one of the investigators, adding yet another layer of complexity to the case.

Throughout the investigation, several suspects were arrested, but these arrests did not advance the investigation. In a notable incident, actor Kai Tanner was taken into custody in July 2007 under unclear circumstances. He spent seven days in detention before Joutsenlahti ordered his immediate release. Tanner later sought compensation from the government for this wrongful arrest and was awarded 11,000 euros.

The investigation took a significant turn in the summer of 2008 when Anneli Orvokki Auer emerged as the main suspect. The police adopted an array of undercover tactics to gather more information about Auer, including wiretapping her phone conversations and surveilling her home. This covert operation began in earnest in April 2009, when Auer crossed paths with Seppo Mäkelä. Unbeknownst to her, Mäkelä was not just an acquaintance; he was an undercover police officer.

Mäkelä ingratiated himself into Auer's life, interacting with her children and making visits to her home. The purpose of this prolonged undercover investigation was to glean insights into Auer's personality and to unearth any potential clues about the night of the murder. It was only during the trial that Auer discovered Mäkelä's true identity. She immediately demanded access to all the information gathered during this clandestine operation. The National Bureau of Investigation (Keskusrikospoliisi, KRP) initially refused her request, arguing that the investigation had not produced any evidence to suggest Auer was the perpetrator. However, Auer eventually succeeded in obtaining all the collected information.

On September 28, 2009, the case took another dramatic turn when Auer was arrested on charges of murdering Lahti. Two days after her arrest, Kuusiranta, a representative of the police, announced that Auer had confessed to the crime. This confession, however, was later retracted by Auer. She claimed that her so-called confession was merely a speculation of scenarios that could have occurred if she were the perpetrator.

Auer herself was baffled by the police's suspicion towards her, especially since she was on the phone with emergency services during the murder. She argued that it would have been nearly impossible for her to simulate the sounds of Lahti's distress that were captured during the call. The emergency call recording became a crucial piece of evidence in the investigation. The police were unable to detect any noises in the recording that could be attributed to an unidentified stranger. During a detailed examination of the emergency call recording, Tuija Niemi, a specialist in sound analysis, made a notable discovery. She isolated a specific utterance made by Anneli Orvokki Auer, when interpreted in the context of the Finnish language, corresponds to the word "kuole", meaning "die".

The investigation took an even more dramatic and unsettling turn in 2011, following a significant development involving the children of Anneli Orvokki Auer and Lahti. The children, who had been placed under the custody of Auer's brother acting as their foster parent, reportedly disclosed new and disturbing details about the night of the murder and other events.

Auer's brother, deeply concerned by these revelations, approached the police with recordings of the children's statements. According to him, the two eldest children provided harrowing accounts of their mother's activities. They alleged that Auer had engaged in Satanic worship rituals that involved the killing of numerous animals. The second eldest child went further, claiming that Auer had been rehearsing the murder of Lahti. They described how Auer had allegedly constructed a wooden shield intended to protect her clothes from blood splatter during the act.

This same child recounted their experience of the murder night, claiming to have overheard the entire event from their room through a door. They described chilling details, such as the sound of a knife being picked up from a table and the pressing of buttons on a record player. The child asserted that the murder occurred before the emergency call was made and that the noises heard during the call were actually from a record player. This assertion was reportedly in agreement with the sound investigator of KRP, who also believed that the murder had taken place before the call.

In 2012, the FBI became involved in the case, analyzing the emergency call recording to determine if it contained manipulated parts, such as pre-recorded segments. Despite their expertise, the FBI found no evidence of tampering with the recording. They also noted their inability to ascertain the number of footsteps or the number of people present in the house based solely on the audio. Contradicting the claims of the second eldest child, the eldest child denied these accusations and maintained that an outsider was responsible for the murder.

This new layer of testimonies and the involvement of international agencies like the FBI added further complexity to an already convoluted case. The conflicting accounts from the children, the eerie details of the alleged rituals and rehearsal, and the inconclusive findings of the FBI's analysis deepened the mystery surrounding Lahti's murder, painting a picture of a case shrouded in uncertainty and eerie allegations.

The trial of Anneli Orvokki Auer, charged with the murder of Jukka S. Lahti, commenced on July 14, 2010, unfolding a dramatic and closely watched legal battle. The prosecution's case was built on the theory that no outsiders were involved in the murder. They argued that Auer, at the climax of a heated argument, killed Lahti and subsequently orchestrated an elaborate staging of the crime scene to mislead investigators.

On November 12, 2010, after an intense trial that gripped public attention, the district court delivered its verdict. Auer was sentenced to life in prison for the murder. Prior to the sentencing, a psychological evaluation was conducted, which concluded that Auer was mentally sound at the time of the murder, a factor that played a significant role in the court's decision.

Unwilling to accept the verdict, Auer challenged the district court's decision in the Court of Appeals in Vaasa. On July 1, 2011, in a surprising turn of events, the Court of Appeals overturned the murder conviction. The acquittal was grounded on several key points raised in Auer's defense. The court considered the testimonies provided by Auer and her eldest child regarding the presence of an outsider, the discovery of bloody footprints, and the mysterious brown fibers found at the crime scene. Additionally, the failure of the police to locate the other weapon purportedly used in the murder cast doubt on the prosecution's narrative.

A critical aspect of the appellate court's decision hinged on the timeline of events on the night of the murder. The court found it implausible that Auer could have had enough time between making the emergency call and the arrival of the first responding officers to stage the entire crime scene by herself. This decision marked a dramatic reversal in the case, raising questions about the evidence, the investigation process, and the challenges in establishing guilt beyond a reasonable doubt in complex criminal cases.

The saga of Anneli Orvokki Auer's legal battles continued with renewed intensity on August 20, 2013, when the case was reopened in court. The prosecutor entered the trial with a bolstered case, claiming that additional investigations had shed light on the motive and events leading up to Jukka S. Lahti's murder. Notably, at the outset of this trial, the prosecution retracted earlier allegations that linked the murder to Satanic worship, a dramatic shift from their previous stance.

On December 12, 2012, the district court of the Satakunta region once again handed down a life sentence to Auer for Lahti's murder. The majority of the judges were convinced that the idea of an outsider being the perpetrator was implausible. They concluded that while the murder was not premeditated, it was executed in an exceptionally cruel and brutal manner.

Undeterred, Auer appealed the decision to the Court of Appeals. On February 19, 2015, in a stunning reversal, the Court of Appeals dismissed the murder charge against her. The appellate court underscored the importance of not allowing innocent individuals to suffer unjustly in the investigation of serious crimes. They found the evidence suggesting an outsider's involvement, coupled with the lack of concrete evidence against Auer, compelling. Additionally, the court expressed skepticism about the reliability of the testimony provided by the youngest children.

Despite the dismissal of the murder charge, Auer's freedom was short-lived, as she faced new allegations. In September 2011, Auer and her new boyfriend were arrested on suspicion of being sexual offenders. On June 29, 2012, the district court of Turku found Auer guilty, sentencing her to seven years in prison for two counts of aggravated rape and three counts of child sexual exploitation. Her ex-boyfriend, Jens Rurik Kukka, born in 1963, received a ten-year sentence for his role in these crimes, which were committed between 2007 and 2009.

Auer and Kukka challenged their convictions, appealing to the Court of Appeals of Turku. On June 27, 2013, the appellate court found Auer additionally guilty of three counts of aggravated assault, extending her sentence by six months to a total of seven years and six months. Kukka's ten-year sentence remained unchanged. The duo then took their case to the European Court of Human Rights (ECHR), seeking further recourse. However, the ECHR declined to investigate their complaints.

This series of trials and appeals, spanning several years, showcased the complexities and twists of a high-profile legal case that captivated public attention. The intertwining of murder and sexual offense charges, the fluctuating verdicts, and the involvement of various courts, including the ECHR, painted a picture of a deeply intricate and controversial legal journey.

Lane Bryant Shooting

On February 2nd, 2008, the small town of Tinley Park, Illinois, nestled about an hour's drive south of the bustling city of Chicago, was enveloped in the chill of winter. The day dawned with a crisp, biting air, as temperatures stubbornly lingered in the mid-20s. The afternoon promised little respite, with the mercury barely nudging above the freezing point. It was the kind of day that coaxed people to seek the warmth and comfort of indoors, away from the icy breath of the Midwestern winter.

Amidst this wintry backdrop, the Lane Bryant store in Tinley Park was set for another day of business. Unbeknownst to many, this day would etch itself into the memory of the community in a profound and unexpected way. Rhoda McFarland, the store manager, was not scheduled to work that morning. Yet, driven by her innate sense of responsibility and leadership, she decided to come in to support her lone employee. This employee, a dedicated 33-year-old nursing student balancing her studies with weekend shifts, had been slated to manage the store's opening single-handedly. Her relief at seeing Rhoda walk through the door that morning was palpable, a silent acknowledgment of the solidarity and teamwork that marked their workplace.

Together, they welcomed the day's first customers as the clock struck 10:00 AM. The store, known for its friendly atmosphere and diverse clothing selection, quickly filled with the muted sounds of shoppers perusing racks and discussing fabric textures and color palettes.

However, the routine of a typical shopping day took a sudden turn with the arrival of a new visitor. A man entered the store, his presence marked by a distinctive appearance: an average height, a husky build, and a unique hairstyle featuring cornrows neatly pulled back, except for one braid adorned with small green beads that dangled over his right ear. His demeanor was friendly, his approach casual, as he struck up a conversation with the staff, exuding the confidence of a delivery man. Clutching a stack of papers, he effortlessly wove his way into the fabric of the store's morning routine.

Yet, something seemed amiss. Rhoda, with her keen managerial instincts, sensed an irregularity. Lane Bryant's delivery schedules were meticulous, and she was acutely aware that no deliveries were expected that day. Her intuition nudging her, Rhoda discreetly made a phone call to a nearby Lane Bryant store, seeking to clarify this unexpected visit. In these crucial moments, her actions reflected a blend of caution and concern, hallmarks of a seasoned manager attuned to the nuances of her environment.

As the minutes ticked by on that fateful morning, the situation inside the Lane Bryant store in Tinley Park took a harrowing turn. The man who had entered under the guise of a delivery person revealed his true intentions in a chilling manner. Suddenly, he brandished a gun, shattering the calm atmosphere of the store. His target was not just the two employees, Rhoda and her colleague whom we'll call "Martha," but also a few unsuspecting customers who had merely come for a routine shopping experience. These women, caught in a terrifying circumstance, found themselves at the mercy of a criminal whose actions were as unpredictable as they were frightening.

The gunman's demands were clear and menacing. He ordered the employees to hand over the store's cash, and didn't stop there. Each woman was compelled to surrender the money they had on them, including the contents of their purses and wallets. He even went so far as to forcibly take any visible jewelry they were wearing, displaying a ruthless disregard for their wellbeing and dignity.

In a more alarming turn, the assailant herded the four women – Rhoda, Martha, and the two customers – into the back of the store, a space typically off-limits to shoppers. The fear and uncertainty of what lay ahead were palpable among the group as they were each bound with duct tape, a sinister preparation by the gunman. Lying face-down and defenseless, the women were subjected to a further violation of their safety when the gunman made a crude and degrading sexual advance towards one of them. This act, while not escalating to full sexual assault, was a demeaning invasion of their personal space and dignity.

In a bizarre and disturbing move, the gunman then took underwear from a store display and placed it over the heads of the four women. This act, seemingly intended to obstruct their vision and prevent them from identifying him or each other, added another layer of fear and humiliation to their ordeal. The women, bound and blindfolded, were left in a vulnerable and terrifying situation, their fate hanging in the balance at the hands of a merciless criminal.

As the ordeal inside the Lane Bryant store continued, the passage of time brought more unsuspecting customers into the fray. Two additional women entered the store, looking to shop for outfits, only to be caught in the midst of the ongoing robbery. They too were confronted by the gunman and coerced at gunpoint to join the others at the back of the store. In a brave but perilous move, one of these women attempted to resist the assailant. Her courage, however, was met with violence; the gunman, in a brutal act of aggression, struck her in the face, likely using his handgun as a weapon. This left her with painful bruises and bloodstains, a physical testament to the severity of the encounter.

The back room of the store, initially a place for inventory and staff activities, had now become a grim holding area for the hostages. The two new captives were quickly subdued, bound with duct tape and articles of clothing, and forced to lie on the floor alongside the first group of women. The tension in the room was palpable, a mix of fear, uncertainty, and a faint glimmer of hope for a resolution.

The situation had been unfolding over an agonizing span of approximately 40 minutes. Initially, the gunman had maintained a semblance of calm and control, but as time wore on, his demeanor began to unravel. It was in this moment of disarray and confusion that Rhoda McFarland, the store manager, recognized a glimmer of opportunity.

With a blend of bravery and quick thinking, Rhoda discreetly used her bluetooth headset to make a crucial call. Her fingers dialed 911, connecting her to the lifeline of emergency assistance. The call was swiftly routed from the Will County Sheriff's Department to the Tinley Park Police, the authority in charge of the area. Although the full details of this desperate whisper for help were never publicly disclosed, snippets of the call revealed Rhoda's urgent request. She managed to convey the location of the distress ("Lane Bryant") and a plea that echoed with both fear and hope: "please hurry." This act of quiet defiance and resourcefulness in the face of danger stood as a beacon of courage.

Just seconds after she discreetly informed the dispatchers, the gunman, realizing her actions, commenced a brutal and deliberate attack on the six hostages, executing them in cold blood. Tragically, five women met an instantaneous and fatal end, but one store employee, through a miraculous twist of fate, narrowly escaped death. In a split-second decision, she turned her head, causing the bullet to merely graze her neck. She feigned death, lying motionless as the gunman hastily fled the scene.

The police, who were astonishingly close by, responded with lightning speed. One officer, already nearby, reached the Lane Bryant store within a minute of Rhoda's call. But the gunman had vanished, leaving behind a harrowing scene. Inside, the officer found the bodies of the five victims and the barely alive survivor. As more police and emergency services rushed in, they declared the tragic fate of the five women while desperately attending to the survivor.

The investigation intensified as law enforcement from Tinley Park and surrounding areas descended on the Brookside Marketplace Shopping Center, a bustling hub with stores like Target and restaurants. Officers meticulously combed through each store, alert and ready, searching for the elusive gunman.

In a dramatic turn, Sean Tyus, a black man innocently waiting in his car in the Target parking lot, became entangled in the investigation. Police, scrutinizing every detail, detained him, examining his shoes and questioning him about his braids, searching for any link to the crime. However, it soon became clear that Sean, like the victims, was just at the wrong place at the wrong time, awaiting his girlfriend who was shopping in Target.

The ensuing hours saw a desperate search by the police, involving helicopters and divers in nearby ponds, hunting for the murder weapon. But the proximity of the shopping center to Interstate 80 raised a chilling possibility – the killer could have easily slipped out of the area, possibly even crossing state lines within the hour.

Among those tragically lost was Rhoda McFarland, a name you might recall from the episode's introduction. At 42, Rhoda's life was full of promise; she had recently become engaged to her fiancé, Stewart, and was looking forward to a bright future. Her sudden passing left a deep scar. In the days following, Rhoda was laid to rest, and a poignant memorial service was held in Crest Hill, where she had once served as a respected pastor. The service, held at the Word of Life Church, saw an overwhelming turnout of 800 mourners. Reverend Tim Bagwell spoke to the gathered crowd about Rhoda, emphasizing the importance of celebrating her life and not letting the tragedy of her death overshadow her legacy. He insisted, "Her death has the ability to overshadow her life, and that should not be. She should not be remembered as a victim."

Sarah Szafranski, the youngest among the victims, was a mere 22 years old when her life was tragically cut short. As the eldest of three siblings, Sarah's journey had been marked by academic achievements at St. Damian's, a private Catholic high school in Oak Forest. She was actively involved in various school clubs and activities, including the Academic Talented Program, Interact Club, Mathletes, Safari, and Spanish Club. Known for her love of board games, Sarah often spent her weekends with her boyfriend, Brian, both sharing a preference for staying in.

Her academic journey led her to Northern Illinois University, where she graduated in May 2007. Sarah was on the cusp of starting a new chapter in her life with a job at CNA Financial Corp. in Chicago. It was in preparation for this new role that she found herself shopping at Lane Bryant for winter work attire. Remembered fondly as a loving, intelligent, and kind-hearted individual, Sarah's loss was deeply felt. Her family, in a statement, encapsulated the profound grief and shock: "Our emotions are raw and we are still in shock. There is nothing adequate anyone can say at a time like this. Sarah was loved by all who knew her and we are counting on that love to sustain us while we mourn."

Carrie Chiuso, hailing from Frankfort, Illinois, was only 33 years old when her life abruptly ended in February 2008. She was the first of the victims to be laid to rest, with her memorial held in Homewood, in the very church where she and her husband, Tony, had exchanged vows less than two years earlier. The couple had been in the midst of planning to start a family in the near future.

Carrie's life was much more than its tragic end. She was a proud alumna of DePaul and Loyola universities, holding both bachelor's and master's degrees. As a social worker, she dedicated herself to supporting at-risk youth, working at the same high school she once attended as a New Kids on the Block fan. Carrie was known for her infectious happiness and her ability to inspire joy in others.

On the day of the tragedy, she had planned to reunite with former DePaul classmates and was shopping at Lane Bryant for a new outfit. Von Mansfield, the principal at Homewood-Flossmore High School where Carrie worked, spoke movingly at her memorial, saying, "Where people are ordinary, Carrie put extra in front of ordinary. She quietly was a part of all that we do," a testament to her extraordinary impact on those around her.

Connie Woolfolk, 37, lived in Flossmoor, Illinois, not far from the tragic incident in Tinley Park. Balancing her life as a single mother, she worked overnight shifts at a nearby Target, and was also building a mortgage company with her mother, who lived with her and her two sons. Her oldest son attended Homewood-Flossmore High School, where Carrie Chiuso, another victim, worked. Connie's younger son, who had spina bifida, required significant care and attention. Those who knew Connie remembered her as someone who expressed love wholeheartedly, and she was fiercely dedicated to providing for her family. She was believed to have fought back against the gunman at Lane Bryant, driven by her strong desire to protect her sons and return to them. Tragically, she sustained severe injuries in the struggle, with evidence suggesting she might have even scratched the gunman, potentially leaving behind DNA evidence.

Jennifer Bishop, 34, an intensive care nurse from South Bend, Indiana, and mother to three young children, was the fifth and final victim. Known for her exceptional care and compassion as a nurse at South Bend's Memorial Hospital, Jeni had been with the hospital for over a decade, working her way up to shift supervisor. On the day of the shooting, she was in Tinley Park with her husband, who was attending a work conference. Jeni decided to visit Lane Bryant, possibly to use a gift card she had received for her recent 34th birthday. Her visit was a coincidental decision that tragically placed her in the path of the gunman. Jeni's untimely death was a profound loss, leaving a void in the lives of her family, colleagues, and the community she served.

Among the victims of the shooting was a miraculous survivor, a 33-year-old part-time employee at Lane Bryant, who was also a nursing student.

Known publicly as "Martha," a pseudonym used by reporters to protect her identity, she endured the harrowing experience and survived by feigning death after being shot in the neck. Immediately treated at the scene, she was swiftly admitted to a hospital and released the next day, but remained under protective custody due to concerns about potential retaliation from the gunman.

In the weeks following the tragedy, "Martha" played a crucial role in the investigation. As the sole eyewitness, her detailed account to the police was instrumental in shaping the understanding of the events that unfolded that tragic Saturday morning. Her contributions added valuable context and insights to the case.

Despite surviving the ordeal, "Martha's" road to recovery was fraught with challenges. She wrote an open letter to the families of the other victims, expressing her profound sorrow and solidarity. In her letter, which was shared with the public by the Tinley Park Police, she conveyed her deepest sympathies to the families and friends of the deceased. She shared that during the terrifying moments of the attack, the thoughts of the victims were on their loved ones and their desire to return home. Expressing her heartache over their inability to do so, she affirmed her commitment to assisting the authorities in any way she could for the sake of all the victims. She also pleaded for privacy for herself and the victims' families in their time of grief and requested that the media respect their need to cope with the aftermath of the crime in private. Lastly, she urged anyone with information that could aid the investigation to come forward, while also asking for understanding regarding her and her family's inability to discuss the events of that day.

Right from the beginning, the Tinley Park Police, led by Sergeant T.J. Grady, classified the tragic shooting at the Lane Bryant store as a robbery gone wrong. This perspective was frequently mentioned in the early stages of the investigation, emphasizing the need for discretion and confidentiality to maintain the integrity of the sensitive case.

As time progressed, it became increasingly evident to investigators that the crime was unlikely to have been motivated by personal vendettas against any of the six women involved – the five victims and the survivor. These women, comprising retail workers, nurses, social workers, as well as mothers, wives, and daughters, led ordinary lives devoid of high-risk elements. Nothing in their backgrounds suggested that they were specifically targeted by the killer.

Moreover, there was no indication that any of the women recognized the assailant. According to the survivor's account, the gunman, who was unmasked during the incident, spent around 40 minutes in the store without any of the women showing signs of familiarity towards him.

One potential lead explored by the investigators was a connection to the church formerly associated with store manager Rhoda McFarland. She had left the church due to disagreements over certain issues, including financial handling. The police pursued this lead as far as Texas, where the church's leadership had moved and acquired land for a new church. However, this line of inquiry seemingly reached a dead end, with no further investigations indicating a link to the crime.

The predominant motive considered in the case was robbery, a theory that has been central from the outset. The gunman not only robbed the Lane Bryant store but also took personal belongings and cash from the victims. He collected around $200 in total, along with some jewelry, as he herded the women to the back of the store.

However, this robbery theory has faced skepticism, particularly due to the nature of the store and the circumstances of the robbery. Lane Bryant, being a relatively affordable clothing chain with most transactions made through credit or debit cards, was not a likely target for a cash-rich heist. Furthermore, the timing of the crime, just after the store's opening at 10:00 AM, raised questions about the amount of cash available on-site. Typically, Lane Bryant stores would make nightly deposits, suggesting limited cash reserves in the morning. Gayle Coolick, a representative from Lane Bryant's parent company, noted the likelihood of low cash levels early in the day.

Some have speculated that the killer might have been a drug addict or someone desperately seeking money, even if it meant resorting to extreme measures for a small amount. The extended duration of the robbery, almost an hour, and the apparent loss of control by the gunman hinted at possible drug use or withdrawal. There's also a possibility that the shooting was not premeditated but a panic response to Rhoda McFarland's 911 call, as the gunman realized the victims had seen his face.

An unnamed law enforcement source, in a discussion with Chicago Sun-Times reporters Frank Main and Annie Sweeney in 2008, suggested that the killer's initial plan was to continue robbing incoming customers. He reportedly intended to take more hostages, rob them, and then confine them in the back room. This plan was presumably disrupted when he noticed McFarland's call for help, leading to the tragic shootings.

While this theory aligns with known details about the killer's actions, it remains speculative without the perpetrator in custody. The true motive, whether it was purely for robbery or influenced by other factors like drug addiction, remains unconfirmed.

A crucial component of the investigation was the testimony of the survivor, the 33-year-old Lane Bryant employee referred to as "Martha" in the media. Living in Mokena and working part-time at the store while studying nursing, she was placed under protective custody following the incident. As the sole eyewitness, her account was invaluable. She provided detailed information on how the gunman entered the store, the sequence of events leading to the women being bound and blindfolded, and the subsequent shootings.

"Martha" also directed the police to a discarded coffee cup, believed to have been used by the gunman on the day of the crime. Although law enforcement has not confirmed the cup's existence, it is speculated that this, along with the blood found under a victim's fingernails, helped identify the gunman's gender and ethnicity. However, no matches to known individuals have been found, suggesting the possibility of the killer having no previous criminal record.

Investigators determined that a .40-caliber semi-automatic Glock handgun was used in the shootings, but the weapon was not left at the scene. Extensive searches in nearby forests, bodies of water, and trash bins failed to turn up the gun or similar ammunition.

One major setback was the lack of security cameras at the Lane Bryant store, eliminating the possibility of obtaining direct footage of the gunman. Nevertheless, the police expanded their search to other nearby businesses and retail establishments, hoping to find security cameras that might have captured the store's vicinity or potential escape routes.

The most significant video evidence in the Lane Bryant shooting case emerged from a nearby Target store in Brookside Marketplace. Although the footage was initially blurry, a collaboration with Dr. David Hathaway and his team at NASA brought crucial details to light. The enhanced video revealed two vehicles, a dark sedan and a larger SUV-type vehicle, arriving at the Lane Bryant store around the time the shooting began.

The timing of these vehicles' arrival and departure was particularly telling. They appeared at 10:39 and 10:40 AM, mere minutes before Rhoda McFarland's 911 call at 10:44 AM, and left shortly after at 10:45 AM, one following the other. This led investigators to speculate that one or both vehicles could be linked to the crime, possibly serving as getaway vehicles for the gunman and potentially an accomplice acting as a lookout.

The nature of the vehicles' arrival and departure suggested a premeditated operation, possibly involving at least three individuals: the shooter and at least two drivers. Whether their motive was a planned robbery or a more personal agenda remains a mystery. What is certain is that within a minute of the tragic shooting, both vehicles had vacated the scene, and the identities of their drivers have remained unknown.

Another pivotal piece of evidence was the 911 call made by store manager Rhoda McFarland on the morning of the shooting. Initially, only a brief segment of this call was shared with the media. However, in the ensuing months, a longer excerpt was released, which provided additional insights, including more details on the gunman's presence and actions during the call.

The gunman was identified as a black man, estimated to be between 25 and 35 years old, with a medium complexion. He was described as having a husky build, broad shoulders, and standing between 5'9" and 6'0" tall, weighing around 200 to 230 pounds. His appearance was characterized by a receding hairline and black hair styled into several puffy cornrows, one of which hung over his right ear and ended with four light-green beads, a distinctive style that led investigators to local salons in search of someone who might recognize him. However, these efforts were unsuccessful.

The man had no visible scars or tattoos and was dressed in a dark winter coat, a dark gray skull cap, and black jeans adorned with rhinestones in the shape of a cursive "G" on the back pocket. A police sketch, created with input from the surviving eyewitness, was released to the public nine days after the shooting, generating over two dozen tips within a day.

Criminal profilers Greg McCrary and Clint Van Zandt, known for their role in identifying the Unabomber, Ted Kaczynski, proposed a profile of the killer. They suggested that he might have been previously incarcerated, and his actions in the Lane Bryant store indicated a determination to avoid returning to prison. They speculated that he may have felt mistreated by society and learned the wrong lessons from his past experiences. One theory was that he might have known or targeted one of the victims, fearing identification, which led him to attack all six women.

McCrary and Van Zandt theorized that the killer's psychology was such that once he had committed one murder, he felt compelled to eliminate all witnesses. They also believed that the gunman was likely to have been involved in further legal troubles or incarcerations since the shooting, and remained a significant danger. Van Zandt emphasized that the gunman would not hesitate to harm anyone he perceived as a threat to his freedom, including close acquaintances or family members.

Over the past decade, the investigation into the Lane Bryant mass murder has remained active, with law enforcement continually pursuing new leads and tips, steadfastly avoiding labeling it as a "cold case." While specific details about the evidence left by the killer, such as fingerprints, DNA, or other forensic clues, have been kept under wraps, it is known that the police have examined a suspect's shoe print on the day of the incident. There is an understanding that the killer's DNA has been obtained, but the exact source and the viability of the sample for forensic comparison remain unclear.

Online speculations suggest the killer might have been a masculine-appearing woman. These theories stem from ambiguities in Rhoda McFarland's 911 call and perceptions of the police sketch. However, such rumors lack substantive evidence. The survivor identified the assailant as male, the voice in the 911 call appears male, and law enforcement has consistently described the shooter as male. If DNA from the killer has been analyzed, it would likely have confirmed the gender and ethnicity.

Despite these online conjectures, there is no solid evidence to support the idea of the killer being a woman. The Tinley Park Police, leading the investigation, have received over 7,500 tips in the 11-plus years since the shooting. The case has seen collaboration with various agencies, including the Illinois State Police, the South Suburban Major Crimes Task Force, the FBI, the Secret Service, Scotland Yard, and NASA, which assisted in enhancing surveillance footage from the nearby Target store. The Vidocq Society, a Philadelphia-based group of former law enforcement experts, was also consulted, but their efforts, like others, did not lead to a resolution.

On the 10-year anniversary of the case in 2018, police released a new 3D image of the gunman, created with the help of the Michigan State Police. This new depiction revitalized interest and led to several tips, but none have successfully led to the identification or apprehension of the perpetrator. As a result, the case remains unsolved, leaving many questions unanswered and justice elusive.

Murder of Lindsay Buziak

Lindsay Elizabeth Buziak, born on November 2, 1983, to parents Jeff Buziak and Evelyn Buziak (née Reitmayer), grew up with her sister Sara, forming a closely-knit family. In 2008, at the age of 24, Lindsay was making impressive strides in her career as a real-estate agent in Victoria. Known for her ambition and talent, she had already established a promising path in her career. Described by those who knew her as both popular and deeply caring, Lindsay's vibrant personality and dedication to her work left a lasting impression on her family, friends, and colleagues.

Her personal life was intertwined with the real estate industry; she was in a relationship with Jason Zailo, who belonged to a well-known and affluent family that operated a successful real estate business. This connection seemingly positioned Lindsay for further success in her field.

However, a peculiar and unsettling event occurred in late January 2008, which raised concerns for Lindsay. She received a phone call from a woman who urgently requested assistance in purchasing a home with a budget of around $1 million. The woman, who spoke with a foreign accent, provided a name that was later suspected to be fictitious. Lindsay was immediately taken aback by the call, especially since she was relatively new to the industry and puzzled about how her personal cell-phone number had been acquired. When questioned, the caller vaguely mentioned that a former client of Lindsay's had shared her contact details.

Troubled by the mysterious nature of the call, Lindsay confided in both her boyfriend, Jason Zailo, and her father, sharing her apprehensions. Despite her unease, Jason saw it as a lucrative opportunity due to the potential high commission from such a significant sale. He encouraged her to proceed with the appointment, offering to provide support by waiting outside the property during the meeting for added safety. Seeking to find the perfect property for this enigmatic client, Lindsay located a suitable home and scheduled a viewing at 5:30 p.m. on Saturday, February 2, 2008. This decision, prompted by a mix of professional ambition and reassurance from her loved ones, led to a series of events that would unfold with unforeseeable and tragic consequences.

On that fateful day, Lindsay Buziak and Jason Zailo shared a late lunch at a local restaurant, a moment of normalcy before the events that would unfold. They settled their bill at 4:24 p.m., then went their separate ways in their vehicles, not knowing that these were some of their last moments of everyday tranquility. Buziak, preparing for her appointment, likely returned home to change her attire, ensuring she presented herself professionally for the high-stakes house viewing. Meanwhile, Zailo, caught up in his own schedule, headed to an automobile repair shop to pick up a colleague, though he was delayed. CCTV footage timestamped 5:30 p.m. captured Zailo leaving the shop, marking his departure towards the rendezvous with Lindsay.

The setting for the appointment, De Sousa Place, was a quaint and quiet cul-de-sac, hosting a mere four houses, a stark contrast to the impending ominous events. Number 1702, the property of interest, sat at the very end of the cul-de-sac, at the junction of De Sousa Place and the busier Torquay Drive. Its side and the fence of the back garden lay parallel to Torquay Drive, giving it a somewhat exposed position to the passersby on the main road.

In a twist to the already mysterious situation, although the caller had assured Lindsay that she would be attending the viewing alone, two individuals were seen approaching the house – a tall, White man with dark hair, and a blond-haired woman, estimated to be between 35 and 45 years old, wearing a dress with a distinctive pattern. This peculiar couple was spotted at 5:30 p.m. by two witnesses, who observed Lindsay greet them. Their handshake, however, seemed formal, suggesting to the onlookers that Lindsay was unfamiliar with the couple – a detail that added an unsettling layer to the meeting.

Jason Zailo, along with his colleague, arrived at the cul-de-sac around 5:40 p.m. As they approached, Zailo glimpsed a figure through the glass of the front door, a sighting that remains shrouded in ambiguity. He parked outside the property, lingering there for about 10 minutes. In an attempt to respect Lindsay's professional space, and not wanting to come across as an overbearing partner, he chose to relocate to another street nearby. After an additional 10 minutes of waiting, filled with growing unease, Zailo sent a text to Lindsay, seeking reassurance that everything was proceeding normally. Tragically, this message went unopened, an ominous sign in the shadow of the events that were unfolding inside the house.

Twenty minutes ticked by, heavy with tension and uncertainty, after Jason Zailo arrived at the property where Lindsay Buziak was conducting her house viewing. Anxious and sensing that something was amiss, Zailo approached the front door, only to find it unyieldingly locked. Peering through the mottled glass of the door, a glimpse of Lindsay's shoes in the entrance hall was the only sign of her presence. The house, eerily silent, offered no response to his persistent knocks. With a growing sense of dread, Zailo made the decisive move to call 9-1-1, seeking urgent help.

At this critical juncture, Zailo's colleague made a pivotal discovery. He noticed a gap in the fence surrounding the back garden. Venturing through, he was met with the startling sight of the back patio door standing wide open – an ominous indication that something was terribly wrong. He quickly alerted Zailo, who, while still on the line with the emergency operator, relayed their intention to enter the house. With a sense of urgency overshadowing caution, Zailo ended the call.

The colleague, navigating through the quiet main level of the house, reached the front door to let Zailo in. The atmosphere was thick with the weight of an unspoken dread as Zailo, propelled by a mix of fear and hope, rushed upstairs. The scene that unfolded in the master bedroom was a tragic tableau – Lindsay Buziak lay in a pool of blood, her life brutally cut short. Zailo, in a state of shock, called 9-1-1 again, this time to report the horrific discovery.

Emergency services arrived swiftly, but it was too late. Lindsay was pronounced dead at the scene. The nature of her injuries was chilling – multiple stab wounds, with an absence of defensive injuries, suggesting a sudden and unexpected attack from behind. In a crime scene marked by violence, it was noted that none of Lindsay's personal belongings were taken, and there was no evidence of sexual assault. The brutality of the act stood in stark contrast to the lack of motive, leaving a haunting question: why had Lindsay Buziak, a young and promising real estate agent, met such a violent and senseless end?

As the minutes inexorably passed, the atmosphere around the property where Lindsay Buziak was conducting her house viewing grew increasingly fraught with unease. Jason Zailo, who had arrived there with the intention of ensuring Lindsay's safety, felt a rising tide of apprehension. Approaching the front door, his unease intensified when he found it stubbornly locked, an unusual occurrence in the context of a house showing. The sight of Lindsay's shoes through the door's mottled glass, so ordinary yet starkly foreboding in their stillness, heightened his concern. The silence that met his knocks at the door was not just absence of sound; it was a heavy, palpable presence, intensifying the sense of something gone terribly wrong. Zailo, grappling with a mix of fear and confusion, made a critical decision to call 9-1-1, hoping for swift assistance.

In a fortuitous turn, Zailo's colleague, who had accompanied him, made a crucial discovery. He found a breach in the fence surrounding the property's back garden. On entering, he was confronted with an alarming sign – the back patio door was conspicuously open. This discovery was an ominous harbinger, suggesting a situation rapidly spiraling out of control. Alerting Zailo to this development, the latter, still communicating with the 9-1-1 operator, conveyed their intent to venture into the house. In this moment, the gravity of the situation necessitated immediate action, overriding the usual caution one might exercise.

Zailo's colleague, threading through the eerily quiet main level of the house, managed to unlock the front door, allowing Zailo to enter. The air inside was thick with a sense of impending doom, a feeling that something tragic had transpired. Driven by a tumultuous mix of fear and faint hope, Zailo ascended the stairs, only to be met with a scene of devastating horror. In the master bedroom lay Lindsay Buziak, tragically and violently robbed of her life, her body in a pool of blood – a stark and gruesome contrast to the life she had lived. Overwhelmed by shock and despair, Zailo placed a second, desperate call to 9-1-1 to report the ghastly scene.

Emergency responders arrived with haste, but their efforts were in vain. Lindsay was declared dead at the scene. The nature of her wounds – multiple stab injuries and a notable absence of defensive wounds – indicated a sudden, treacherous attack from behind, leaving no chance for resistance. In a setting marred by such brutality, the fact that none of Lindsay's possessions were missing and there was no sign of sexual assault only deepened the mystery. The violence of the crime starkly contrasted with the apparent lack of motive, leaving those who knew her, and the community at large, grappling with how Lindsay Buziak, a vibrant and aspiring young real estate agent, could have met with such a cruel and senseless demise.

The investigation led to a complex web of connections and potential leads, one of which involved Jason Zailo's family, primarily due to their ties with the location of the crime – De Sousa Court. Named after Joe De Sousa, a developer and business associate of Shirley Zailo, Jason's mother, the cul-de-sac became a focal point in the case. At the time of the murder, parts of the cul-de-sac were still under construction, and it was reported that De Sousa himself was present at the site supervising construction work just an hour before the murder occurred. This proximity in time and space inevitably cast a spotlight on the Zailo family, prompting investigators to delve into their potential involvement. However, despite these connections and the scrutiny they invited, the police eventually clarified that no member of the Zailo family was considered a suspect in the case.

In September 2010, the American network NBC aired an episode of "Dateline" titled "Dream House Murder," which shed light on new aspects of the investigation. It was revealed that approximately eight weeks before her murder, while on a visit to Calgary in December 2007, Lindsay Buziak had attempted to contact a friend of her ex-boyfriend. Intriguingly, this friend was arrested on January 22, 2008, during what was the largest drug bust in Alberta's history, accused of being a significant figure in a drug-trafficking operation. This arrest led to speculation that Lindsay's murder might have been a hit ordered by a drug cartel, under the belief that she was a police informant. However, Saanich detectives, along with crime scene investigator Yolanda McClary and veteran homicide detective Dwayne Stanton, quickly dismissed this theory. They concluded that Lindsay was not an informant and that the nature of her murder – brutal yet seemingly amateurish – did not align with the methods typically employed by hired killers associated with drug cartels.

The investigators were also drawn to another potential lead involving a separate drug bust. This involved a man whose phone had been tapped due to his significant role in drug trafficking in British Columbia and Alberta. These wiretaps had previously led to notable raids, including those at the BC Legislature in 2003. Intriguingly, Lindsay's and her boyfriend's phones were also tapped, ostensibly due to his association with this group. Yet, this lead too was eventually set aside. Lindsay had no known involvement in drug use or trafficking, and she was not listed as a witness in the subsequent trial.

These investigations painted a picture of a complex, multi-faceted inquiry, where personal connections, professional ties, and coincidental associations were exhaustively explored. Yet, in the midst of these numerous leads and theories, the true motive and identity of Lindsay Buziak's killer remained shrouded in mystery. The investigators leaned towards a belief that the murder was a highly personal act, orchestrated by someone within Lindsay's close circle, possibly with access to inside information from her real-estate office.

As the investigation continued through 2008, a chilling account emerged from Nikki, a close friend of Lindsay. Nikki recounted a disturbing experience that occurred sometime after the murder. She was jolted awake by a mysterious phone call in the middle of the night, coming from an unknown number. Groggily answering, she heard a female voice on the other end, speaking with a peculiar accent that Nikki couldn't quite identify. The details of the conversation were hazy in Nikki's memory, but the unusual accent struck a nerve. She remembered Lindsay mentioning that her unidentified client, who was now a prime suspect in the murder, had spoken with a strange, possibly feigned accent. This eerie similarity sent a shiver of fear down Nikki's spine.

Driven by a mix of curiosity and alarm, Nikki attempted to call back the mysterious number repeatedly, "20 or 30 times," until finally, she received a response. To her surprise, it was Shirley Zailo, the mother of Lindsay's boyfriend, Jason, who answered. Confused and concerned, Nikki questioned Shirley about the reason for the call and how she had obtained her number, considering they were not acquainted. Shirley's response was that she had meant to call her secretary, who coincidentally was also named Nikki. She speculated that Jason might have added the other Nikki's number to her contacts by mistake. However, Shirley Zailo has denied that this incident ever took place, and it remains unclear whether authorities investigated Nikki's claim further.

Each February, in a poignant tribute to Lindsay, her father Jeff leads an annual walk to commemorate her life and to keep her case in the public's consciousness. This solemn tradition reflects the ongoing quest for justice and the enduring impact of Lindsay's loss on her family and community.

Adding to the case's complexity, in August 2017, a startling comment appeared on a message board of the investigative website run by Jeff Buziak. An anonymous individual brazenly claimed responsibility for Lindsay's murder, taunting that the police would never be able to prove it. This disturbing proclamation only added more layers to the already convoluted case.

In 2020, the Capital Daily delved deeper into the case, requesting the release of public records. Their report brought to light previously undisclosed details, including the police's knowledge of two phones used by the suspects – one with a Vancouver number, solely used to contact Lindsay, and another used to check the voicemail of the first phone. Additionally, they uncovered unusual Internet activity linked to Lindsay before her murder and initial police suspicions that violent criminals among her Facebook friends might have been involved.

In a glimmer of hope, February 2021 saw the Saanich police announce that advancements in DNA analysis and other technologies had led to new leads in the case. However, as time marches on without further updates, the shadow of doubt looms larger, casting a bleak outlook on whether this complex and heart-wrenching case will ever be resolved.

Noida Double Murder

Aarushi Talwar, born on May 24, 1994, was a bright and aspiring 13-year-old student at Delhi Public School. She was the cherished daughter of Dr. Rajesh Talwar and Dr. Nupur Talwar, both respected dentists. The Talwars resided in a welcoming apartment located in the bustling Sector 25 (Jalvayu Vihar) of Noida, Uttar Pradesh, a region known for its vibrant community and cultural diversity.

Dr. Rajesh and Dr. Nupur Talwar were not only partners in life but also in their profession. Together, they ran a successful dental clinic in Sector 27 of Noida, a place where they devotedly provided care to their patients. Dr. Rajesh Talwar also played a significant role at Fortis Hospital, leading the dental department with his expertise and passion. His commitment to education was evident through his teaching role at the ITS dental college in Greater Noida, where he inspired many young minds.

The Talwars were closely knit with another dentist couple, Anita and Praful Durrani, who were not only their close friends but also their professional associates. The Durranis and the Talwars shared a strong bond, both personally and professionally. They jointly operated the Noida clinic, where Dr. Rajesh and Dr. Anita managed the morning sessions, while Dr. Praful and Dr. Nupur looked after the evening appointments. Their collaboration extended to another clinic situated in the picturesque Hauz Khas area of Delhi, demonstrating their deep-rooted partnership and mutual respect.

In the heart of the Talwar household was Yam Prasad Banjade, affectionately known as Hemraj. He was the family's trusted live-in domestic help and a skilled cook, hailing from the serene Dharapani village in the Arghakhanchi district of Nepal. Hemraj's journey to India began in the 1980s, driven by his quest for better opportunities. He joined the Talwar family seven months before his untimely demise. Born in January 1963, as indicated by his passport, Hemraj's actual age was thought to be higher, hinting at a life filled with experiences and stories from a land far away.

Together, these individuals formed a tapestry of relationships and professional alliances, each playing a unique role in the shared narrative of their lives in Noida. Their stories, interwoven with personal dreams and professional aspirations, paint a vivid picture of a community bound by more than just geographical proximity.

On the evening of May 15, 2008, the sequence of events that led up to the tragic night began unfolding in the Talwar household. Nupur Talwar spent her morning working at her clinic and later picked up Aarushi from school at 1:30 PM, returning to their Jalvayu Vihar apartment for lunch. They were joined by Vandana Talwar, Rajesh's sister-in-law. Post-lunch, Nupur left for Fortis Hospital, where she worked until 7 PM, while Aarushi stayed back at home. Meanwhile, Rajesh Talwar was engaged at the ITS Dental College, teaching until 3:30 PM, followed by attending patients at his clinic until 8:30 PM.

The evening progressed as Rajesh and his driver, Umesh Sharma, arrived back at Jalvayu Vihar around 9:30 PM. Sharma, after dropping Rajesh, parked the car at Nupur's parents' house nearby and returned to hand over the car keys and Rajesh's bag to Hemraj, the family's domestic help. At this time, Sharma saw Nupur and Aarushi near the dining table and Rajesh emerging from his bedroom. This moment marked the last known sighting of Aarushi and Hemraj by someone outside the family.

As the night moved towards 10 PM, the Talwars presented Aarushi with an early birthday gift – a Sony DSC-W130 digital camera, which had arrived earlier that day and was enthusiastically used by Aarushi to take several photographs of herself and her parents. Subsequently, Aarushi's parents retired to their room, while she remained in hers.

Closer to 11 PM, Rajesh requested Nupur to activate the internet router located in Aarushi's room. Upon entering, Nupur observed Aarushi reading 'The 3 Mistakes of My Life' by Chetan Bhagat. After switching on the router, Nupur returned to her room. Around the same time, Rajesh attended a phone call from the US, indicating that the ringer was not on silent mode. He later engaged in browsing stock market and dentistry-related websites and sent an email, with the last internet usage recorded at 11:41:53 PM.

The early hours of May 16 saw Aarushi's friend Anmol trying to reach her on her mobile phone and the Talwar residence's landline, but to no avail. He also sent an SMS, which Aarushi's phone did not receive. The internet router was last used at 12:08 AM. The sequence of events from midnight to 6:00 AM remains a mystery, but the post-mortem reports indicated that both Aarushi and Hemraj were killed between 12:00 AM and 1:00 AM.

The Talwar's 1300 sq. ft. apartment consisted of three bedrooms, including the servant's quarters, a drawing-dining room, and a separate room for Hemraj. Rajesh and Nupur occupied the master bedroom, while Aarushi had an adjacent room. Hemraj's room had two access points: one from outside the apartment and another connecting internally. The main entrance to the apartment was secured by three doors: a grill gate, a mesh door, and a wooden door, all attached to the same frame. Hemraj's room also had a door positioned between the two grill doors at the entrance. Interestingly, the outermost grill gate was removed by the Talwars a year after the murders.

On the morning of May 16, 2008, a routine day began to unravel into a scene of tragedy at the Talwar household. The family's housemaid, Bharati

Mandal, aged 35 and recently employed, approached the house around 6 am, a time when the residence was typically still in slumber. Normally, Hemraj, the domestic help, would open the door for her, but on this day, repeated ringing of the doorbell brought no response. She even attempted to push the outermost gate, but found it unyielding.

After her third attempt, Nupur Talwar opened the innermost wooden door. Speaking through the mesh grill, Nupur expressed surprise that the door was locked from the outside, inquiring if Bharati had seen Hemraj. Nupur speculated that Hemraj might have stepped out to buy milk, inadvertently locking the door from outside, and asked Bharati to wait for his return. Bharati, reluctant to wait, requested the spare keys. Nupur agreed and asked her to move downstairs to catch the keys thrown from the balcony.

During this exchange, Nupur attempted to call Hemraj's mobile, only to be met with an abrupt disconnection and subsequent unavailability. Downstairs, Bharati insisted on receiving the keys regardless of the door's status, to avoid another climb up the stairs. Nupur complied and tossed the keys down to her.

By now, Rajesh Talwar had awoken and stumbled upon a disconcerting sight in the living room – an almost empty bottle of Scotch whisky on the dining table. His confusion quickly turned to alarm, prompting Nupur to check Aarushi's room. They found her room, typically locked and only accessible from inside or with a key, unlocked. The harrowing discovery of Aarushi's lifeless body on her bed left Rajesh in an outcry and Nupur in a state of shock.

Meanwhile, Bharati found that the outermost gate, previously immovable, now opened easily. Inside, she discovered the middle door latched but not locked. Entering the apartment, she encountered the grieving parents. Nupur beckoned her into Aarushi's room, where Bharati stood at the threshold, witnessing the grim scene of Aarushi covered with a flannel blanket. When Nupur unveiled the blanket, Aarushi's slit throat was revealed, leading the parents to immediately accuse Hemraj of the murder.

After informing the neighbors of the tragedy, Bharati returned, only to be dismissed from her duties for the day by the distraught Talwars. In the meantime, the news of the murder in the upscale neighborhood spread rapidly, drawing family, friends, and media to the house. By the time police arrived, the living room was crowded with about 15 people, and the bedroom had 5-6 people, leaving Aarushi's room as the only vacant space. The crime scene was significantly disturbed by the influx of people, complicating the investigation that was to follow.

On May 16, the Talwars' missing servant, Hemraj, became the primary suspect in the case. Rajesh Talwar, in his police complaint, accused Hemraj of murdering his daughter. He urged the police to focus their efforts on finding Hemraj, even offering 25,000 rupees to expedite the search to Hemraj's native village in Nepal. The police theorized that Hemraj, possibly under the influence of alcohol, attempted to sexually assault Aarushi and killed her with a kukri, a Nepalese knife, when she resisted. A reward of ₹20,000 was announced for information leading to Hemraj's capture.

The day proceeded with Aarushi's body being sent for a post-mortem examination around 8:30 am, accompanied by Rajesh's brother Dinesh, driver Umesh Sharma, and a childhood friend, Ajay Chadha. The body was returned home at 1 pm and placed on ice slabs in the living room before being taken for cremation at 4 pm. The Talwars, later accused of hastening the cremation, defended their actions by citing the body's rapid decomposition and pressure from family elders, alongside police confirmation that the body was no longer needed for examination.

The police later criticized the Talwars' household staff for cleaning Aarushi's room too quickly. However, the Talwars' compounder, Vikas Sethi, testified that he had received permission from the police and a lady constable at the scene to clean the house.

During the cleanup, a section of Aarushi's blood-stained mattress was cut and sent for forensic analysis along with her pillow, bedsheet, and clothes. Sethi, along with others, attempted to dispose of the remaining mattress but found the terrace locked. Directed by a neighbor to use the adjacent terrace, they asked Puneesh Tandon, the neighbor, for access. Earlier in the day, the ice used for Aarushi's body had also been disposed of on this terrace. Unbeknownst to them, Hemraj's body lay on the neighboring terrace, unseen due to a dividing grilled wall.

Simultaneously, a series of phone conversations occurred among Dinesh Talwar, Dr. Sushil Chaudhury (Dinesh's friend and chairman of ICARE Eye Hospital), and K K Gautam, a retired Deputy Superintendent of Police, while the post-mortem report was being prepared. Gautam later testified in court that Chaudhury had requested him to omit any references to sexual assault from the post-mortem report, a request he refused. He mentioned this incident to the first CBI team, but it was not recorded in their files.

On the morning of May 16, some visitors at the Talwars' house noticed bloodstains on the handle of the terrace door. Rajesh Talwar's former colleagues, Rajiv Kumar Varshney and Rohit Kochhar, informed the police about seeing these stains on the terrace door, its lock, and the staircase leading to the terrace. Varshney had accidentally taken the stairs to the terrace during his visit. However, several other witnesses, including police officers, Umesh Sharma, Puneesh Rai Tandon, Bharati Mandal, and Vikas Sethi, reported not seeing any bloodstains on the staircase that morning. This discrepancy led to speculation that the bloodstains might have been left by those attempting to move Aarushi's mattress to the terrace.

Kochhar mentioned that the stains were pointed out to a police constable, Akhilesh Kumar, but initially, the policeman dismissed the mark on the terrace door as rust and overlooked the bloodstains on the floor. Varshney recalled the police suggesting that the killer might have tried to escape or hide a weapon on the terrace but found it locked. Despite these observations, when the police were persuaded to investigate the terrace, they couldn't access it due to a missing key. According to testimonies, when asked for the key, Rajesh Talwar went inside the house and did not return for a long time. Rajesh later stated that he couldn't recall the exact events but insisted he never hindered the investigation. The police eventually left the terrace door locked until the next day, citing their inability to find the key or a mechanic to break open the door.

On the morning of May 17, while Rajesh and Nupur Talwar went to Haridwar to immerse Aarushi's ashes in the Ganges, the house was managed by Dinesh Talwar. Among the visitors was retired police officer K.K. Gautam, who was shown the bloodstains on the terrace door handle by Dinesh. Gautam then called SP Mahesh Mishra, who sent an officer to the scene. With the terrace key still missing, the officer broke open the lock. Upon entering, they discovered bloody drag marks and a decomposed body lying in a pool of blood around 10:30 am.

Unable to identify the body, Dinesh called Rajesh and Nupur, asking them to return. When the couple arrived, Nupur stayed in the car with Aarushi's ashes, while Rajesh went to identify the body. He couldn't confirm if it was Hemraj due to the extent of injuries and decomposition, but later a friend of Hemraj identified it as his.

After the identification, Rajesh and Nupur continued their journey to Haridwar, where Rajesh recorded Aarushi's death time as 2 am in the priest's records. An autopsy of Hemraj's body was conducted that night by Dr. Naresh Raj.

The crime scene at the Talwar residence was not immediately secured by the Uttar Pradesh police, leading to significant contamination. Numerous individuals, including members of the media, were allowed to roam freely through the apartment, greatly compromising the integrity of the evidence. The forensic team, upon their arrival, faced a challenging situation as nearly 90% of the crucial evidence had already been destroyed due to this oversight.

Post-mortem reports of Aarushi and Hemraj indicated that both victims died between 12 am and 1 am. The initial cause of death for both was attributed to blunt force trauma, evidenced by a "U/V-shaped" injury, which was followed by the slitting of their throats with a sharp object. There were no signs of asphyxia.

In the initial forensic analysis conducted in May 2008, it was determined that Aarushi had been struck with a heavy, sharp-edged weapon. The first blow to her forehead was fatal, leading to her death within two minutes, as suggested by the size of the blood clot.

However, in 2012, after Aarushi's parents were accused of her murder, the CBI presented a new theory. They suggested that the dimensions of the injuries on both bodies matched the "striking distance" of one of Rajesh Talwar's golf clubs. Dr. Sunil Dohre, part of the investigation, testified that a golf club could have been the weapon used to inflict the U/V-shaped injuries. The defense, however, challenged this claim, arguing that the CBI officers influenced Dr. Dohre to mention the "golf club." Additionally, the Talwars' lawyer presented forensic expert Dr. RK Sharma, who testified that the hairline fracture found on Aarushi could not have been caused by a golf club, further complicating the case.

The murder weapon used to slit the throats of Aarushi and Hemraj was never recovered. Forensic analysis revealed that the precise and identical nature of the lacerations on both victims suggested the use of the same weapon. Forensic scientists noted in May 2008 that the wounds were inflicted with clinical precision, targeting the windpipe and the vital left common carotid artery, which supplies oxygenated blood to the brain.

Initially, the Noida police, suspecting the parents, hypothesized that a "surgical knife" might have been the murder weapon. However, by June 2008, the CBI shifted suspicion to three Nepali men and speculated the weapon to be a kukri, a traditional Nepali knife. Later, the second CBI team revisited the "surgical instrument" theory, suggesting that the Talwars, being dental professionals trained in surgery, could have used a surgical scalpel. The defense countered this by stating that a dentist's scalpel, usually delicate and about a centimeter in cutting surface, would be incapable of cutting through the carotid artery. Defense witness Dr. RK Sharma suggested that the injuries could have been caused either by surgical scalpel No. 10, which is not typically used by dentists, or a kukri.

At the crime scene, Aarushi's body was found on her bed, covered with a white flannel blanket and her face obscured by her schoolbag. Despite blood on the pillow, bed, walls, floor, and the bedroom door, there was no blood on the toys, schoolbag, or the pink pillow at the back of the bed. These items, within the range of the blood splatter, seemed to have been placed on the bed post-murder. The book 'The 3 Mistakes of My Life', which Aarushi was reportedly reading, was found without bloodstains.

The 2008 post-mortem report noted a "whitish discharge" in Aarushi's genital area but no signs of sexual assault. This discharge was examined at a local hospital and found to be devoid of semen. However, concerns arose in 2009 when the sample sent to the CBI's forensic labs was suspected of being tampered with, although it was later concluded to be contaminated, not tampered.

The bed sheet under Aarushi had a wet circular mark, not attributable to urine, as her lower garments appeared disturbed. The CBI suspected her pelvic area was wiped clean, and her pyjamas adjusted post-mortem.

In a controversial later statement in 2012, Dr. Dohre described Aarushi's private parts as "extraordinarily dilated" with no signs of rape, noting a ruptured hymen and an "unduly large" vaginal orifice. He suggested that these findings, which he initially omitted due to their subjective nature, indicated post-mortem manipulation of the body. The complexity of these findings added further layers of ambiguity to an already convoluted and tragic case.

Evidence from the crime scene suggested that Hemraj's body had been dragged about 20 feet on the terrace after his death. This conclusion was drawn from the blood trail found on the terrace and the abrasion-contusion marks on his elbows.

Hemraj's body was discovered to the left of the roof entrance, near the external unit of an air conditioner (AC). The body was partially covered with a panel from a roof cooler. The distribution of blood near the AC unit indicated that the body had likely been dragged in that direction. Experts from the Forensic Science Laboratory in Gandhinagar and the Central Forensic Science Laboratory concluded that the drag mark was consistent with a blood-soaked body being moved while wrapped in a bed sheet. This raised the possibility that Hemraj was murdered elsewhere and then moved to the terrace. However, a UV Light testing team from the CBI reported in June 2008 that Hemraj's bloodstains were only found on the terrace, suggesting the murder may have actually taken place there. The blood found on the staircase on May 17 could have been transferred from the mattress the cleaners were attempting to move to the terrace.

Additional clues included a double-bed cover draped over the iron grill separating the Talwars' terrace from the neighboring one, and a smudged blood-stained palm print on the terrace wall, identified as Hemraj's blood but with an unidentifiable print. A blood-stained shoe print, estimated to be size 8 or 9, was also documented by the police.

The Talwars' lawyer, Pinaki Mishra, mentioned that those who discovered Hemraj's body observed hair in his mouth, potentially belonging to the killer. However, this detail was reportedly not investigated by the police.

In contrast to Aarushi, whose body contained undigested food, Hemraj's stomach only had about 25 ml of liquid, suggesting he hadn't eaten dinner.

This observation was corroborated by the untouched dinner found in the kitchen on the morning of May 16.

During the 2012 court proceedings against Aarushi's parents, Dr. Naresh Raj testified that Hemraj's penis was swollen when the body was brought in for autopsy, implying a potential sexual context. However, the defense lawyer referenced medical literature stating such swelling can be a normal post-mortem occurrence. Dr. Raj countered by admitting his conclusion was not based on medical authority but rather on personal experience from his married life, casting doubt on the scientific basis of his observation.

On July 1, 2008, KK Gautam provided a statement to the first CBI team regarding his observations in Hemraj's room on May 17. He reported seeing three glasses, two with some liquor and one empty, alongside three bottles: Kingfisher beer, Sprite, and Sula whisky. DNA from Hemraj was later found on the Kingfisher bottle, despite CBI investigators noting that he was reportedly a teetotaler.

Gautam also noted the presence of urine from more than one person in the servant's toilet and a depression on Hemraj's mattress, suggesting the possibility of three people in the room. However, in 2012, he contradicted this earlier statement, denying that there was any liquor in the glasses and that he hadn't implied the presence of three people based on the mattress's state. He accused an officer from the first CBI team of distorting his statement to fit their investigation narrative.

The apartment showed no signs of forced entry, and the middle grill door was found latched from outside on the morning of May 16. The Talwars and Hemraj had keys to the house. On that morning, Nupur Talwar threw a bunch of keys to the maid, Bharati, which she claimed were her own as she couldn't find Hemraj's keys.

The maid, Bharati, initially couldn't open the outermost gate but managed to do so after retrieving the keys thrown by Nupur. The CBI theorized that the gate was initially latched from inside and was unlatched by Nupur through Hemraj's room. However, Bharati later testified in court that the door was only latched, not locked, which the defense supported by presenting Rajesh's driver, Umesh Sharma, as a witness.

The key to the terrace door, believed to be with Hemraj's keys, was never found after the murders. The door to Aarushi's room and the main door of the house locked automatically. On the morning of May 16, the key to Aarushi's room was found on a framed wall sculpture near the house entrance. Nupur stated that she might not have properly closed Aarushi's door the last time she entered or might have left the keys in the key slot. She maintained this claim across various tests.

In 2013, SP Mahesh Kumar Mishra testified that Rajesh Talwar had informed him that he locked Aarushi's room from outside at 11:30 pm on the night of the murder but had forgotten to lock his own bedroom door, suggesting that the key to Aarushi's room could have been taken from there.

Both Aarushi and Hemraj had mobile phones that went missing after the murder. Hemraj's phone was a Tata Indicom handset, electronically registered as #20CFA3EC, with the SIM card in Rajesh Talwar's name. On May 15, Hemraj received two calls from the Talwars' clinic; Rajesh was at his Hauz Khas clinic and Nupur was at Fortis Hospital in Noida, as confirmed by their mobile phone records. The defense lawyer later suggested that Krishna Thadarai, an employee, was at the Noida clinic during these calls.

The last call to Hemraj was made at 8:27 pm, lasting 6 minutes, from a PCO about a kilometer away from the Talwars' apartment. The caller's identity remained unknown. The following morning, Nupur called Hemraj from their landline at 6:01 am; the call was abruptly disconnected. The phone, at that time, was within the coverage area of the Nithari village cell tower, which also covered the Talwars' apartment complex. Hemraj's phone was never recovered but was reportedly briefly active in Punjab later.

Aarushi used a gloss black Nokia N72 and was usually in contact with friends until after midnight. However, on the night of May 15, her phone became inactive after 9:10 pm. Her friend Anmol tried to reach her later that night, both on her mobile and the family's landline, without success. An SMS sent around midnight was not received by Aarushi's phone.

Days after Aarushi's death, her phone was discovered on a dirt track near Noida's Sadarpur area by a housemaid, Kusum. Her brother, Ram Bhool, had been in possession of the phone since May 2008 but began using it only in February 2009 with a new SIM card. The police eventually traced the phone to Bulandshahar, recovering it from Jitender, who had recently purchased it from Ram Bhool. Kusum and Ram Bhool were detained for questioning, but the CBI concluded they were unaware of the phone's connection to Aarushi and had no involvement in the murders. The phone was found without a data card, pictures, or text messages.

The Talwars' landline phone, kept in Rajesh and Nupur Talwar's bedroom, became a focal point in the investigation. Anmol, a friend of Aarushi, called the landline around 11:30 pm, and the call lasted 34 seconds, but Rajesh denied knowledge of this call. Anmol also tried the landline around midnight after failing to reach Aarushi on her mobile, but there was no response. The Talwars suggested that Aarushi might have turned off the landline ringer that night.

Puneesh Tandon, a neighbor, testified in court that he inquired about a police call on the morning of May 16, but was told by Nupur's father that the landline was out-of-order.

Rajesh Talwar's mobile phone records indicated he was at his residence on the night of the murder. He made various professional calls until 11:01 pm, and his next call was recorded at 6:19 am the following day, after Aarushi's body was discovered. Nupur's mobile was switched off from the evening of

May 15 until the afternoon of May 18, and records showed it had not been turned off in the 60 days preceding the murder.

Hemraj had reportedly expressed concerns about a threat to his life to his friends. Usha Thakur, a social worker, confirmed Hemraj shared his fears for his and others' safety five days before his murder, but she couldn't assist him due to a family emergency.

Three years after the murder, in March 2011, Hemraj's wife Khumkala came from Nepal to India and filed a plea in the CBI court in Ghaziabad, suspecting the Talwars of the murders. She alleged strained relations between Hemraj and Rajesh, recounting Hemraj's description of Rajesh as short-tempered and threatening. She claimed Hemraj had phoned her 15 days before his murder, saying the Talwars suspected him of leaking family secrets and threatened him. She also mentioned Hemraj's dissatisfaction with his job and his unsuccessful attempt to send money home since December 2007, alleging the Talwars withheld his dues after his murder. When asked about her delayed revelations, she expressed her initial faith in the Indian judiciary and cited her lack of awareness due to her family's poor background.

Hemraj had seemingly prepared his dinner around 10:30 pm but did not consume it, as indicated by his untouched plate and tidy bed, suggesting he did not sleep that night. A Ballantine's Scotch whisky bottle with bloodstains of both Aarushi and Hemraj was discovered on the dining table. The bottle, originating from a concealed mini-bar in the house, implied that the individual handling it was familiar with the house's layout. Seized on the morning of May 16, no clear fingerprints could be retrieved from the bottle.

Crime scene photographs and fingerprint collection were conducted by Constable Chunnilal Gautam on May 16. Out of 26 fingerprints collected, 24 were improperly preserved, leaving only two viable for analysis, which did not match any suspects. Notably, Aarushi's fingerprints were not taken.

Regarding Aarushi's camera, photos numbered 13, 15, 20, 22, and 23 were found, indicating that at least 23 photos were taken, with 18 deleted. The CBI speculated that someone other than Aarushi might have deleted these photos, but Nupur suggested that Aarushi could have deleted undesirable shots herself.

The internet router in Aarushi's room, which turned off at around 3:43 am, about three hours post the estimated time of Aarushi's murder, was noted by the CBI. A CERT-In technical expert stated that the router's activity indicated either a power cut or manual intervention; no power cut was reported that night. Despite this, the router's intermittent activity on May 16 rendered it an unreliable piece of evidence.

The initial police investigation faced criticism for focusing on Hemraj as the prime suspect and for procedural lapses, such as not securing the crime scene. These oversights led to the reassignment of the investigating officer, Inspector Dataram Nauneria, and the transfer of Superintendent of Police Mahesh Mishra.

On May 19, the police considered Vishnu Sharma, a former Nepali domestic helper and clinic assistant of the Talwars, as a suspect. Vishnu, who introduced Hemraj to the Talwars as his temporary replacement but lost his job upon returning, was suspected of harboring a grudge against Hemraj and possibly murdering Aarushi as a witness. However, no evidence linked Vishnu to the murders, and he was confirmed to have been in Nepal on the day of the incident.

By May 21, the investigation into the murders saw the Delhi Police joining forces with the Uttar Pradesh Police. Several factors began to raise suspicion towards Aarushi's parents. Despite the close proximity of their bedrooms, only 7-8 feet apart, the parents claimed they didn't hear any disturbance and slept through the murders. Furthermore, there was no evidence of forced entry into Aarushi's room, which was typically locked at night. The key to her room, usually kept beside Nupur's bed, was inexplicably found in the living room after the murder.

Rajesh Talwar's behavior also attracted attention. On the morning following the murders, he urged the police to pursue Hemraj, even offering to finance their trip to Hemraj's village in Nepal, which was seen as a potential diversion tactic. Rajesh's reluctance to provide the key to the terrace door, coupled with efforts to conceal Hemraj's body, raised further doubts. The body was covered with a cooler panel, and a bed sheet obscured the adjacent terrace's iron grill. This led to a suspicion that the Talwars planned to blame Hemraj for Aarushi's murder and dispose of his body later.

The condition of the crime scene suggested alteration. Aarushi's bed sheet remained smooth, and her body was covered with a white flannel blanket. Significantly, items like her toys, schoolbag, and a pink pillow, free of bloodstains, seemed to have been placed in the room post-murder. The family was also accused of showing undue haste in cremating Aarushi and cleaning the crime scene on May 16.

Observers, including visitors and SP Mahesh Kumar Mishra, noted the parents' lack of expected shock or grief. Mishra specifically mentioned that the Talwars appeared very nervous during questioning. Adding to the intrigue were telephonic conversations between May 16 and 17 involving KK Gautam, Dr. Sushil Chaudhury, and Rajesh's brother Dinesh Talwar. Gautam later alleged that Chaudhury had attempted to influence the post-mortem report to remove any reference to sexual assault.

Compounding these suspicions, Hemraj had previously voiced concerns about a threat to his life, possibly linked to his knowledge of Rajesh's alleged extramarital affair. Based on these accumulated suspicions, the police started focusing on the parents as prime suspects. On May 22, Inspector-General Gurdarshan Singh proposed a theory where Rajesh, blackmailed by Hemraj over an alleged affair, killed Hemraj on the terrace and then Aarushi, who was a witness. Singh emphasized that arrests would only be made with conclusive evidence.

On May 23, Rajesh and Nupur Talwar were separated for questioning. Nupur was placed in a room with her cousin and a woman constable, while Rajesh was arrested and presented before a local magistrate, followed by his transfer to Dasna jail. Rajesh claimed that he was coerced into signing a confession and threatened with harm by the police, who also allegedly considered killing him. Since it was a Friday, he couldn't apply for bail until Monday and spent the weekend in jail.

That same day, Inspector-General Gurdarshan Singh held a press conference where he publicly accused Rajesh of murdering Aarushi and Hemraj to conceal his extramarital affair with Anita Durrani. Singh suggested that Aarushi had objected to her father's affair and might have confided in or even developed a relationship with Hemraj. He outlined a sequence of events where Rajesh, upon finding Aarushi and Hemraj in an "objectionable" position, killed them both. Singh later altered his theory under criticism, suggesting Aarushi was killed when she confronted her father about the affair, and Hemraj was a witness. Nupur was accused of helping to cover up the crime, and Rajesh was said to have made a confession, which he denied.

Public opinion turned against the Talwars, leading to Rajesh's dismissal from Fortis Hospital. However, many in the Indian Dental Association and his former patients continued to believe in his innocence.

The police also seized Rajesh's laptop and Aarushi's computer hard disk. They released selective emails to portray Aarushi as having strained relations with her father, though these were often taken out of context or misinterpreted. Media reports further sensationalized the case, with claims about the Talwars' involvement in wife-swapping and attending high-society parties, all of which were refuted by Nupur and the CBI.

The character assassination of Aarushi and her family, particularly the insinuation of a sexual relationship with Hemraj, caused outrage among her friends and relatives. Supporters condemned the police and media for depicting Aarushi as a promiscuous teenager, using innocuous details like receiving flowers, a school project on drug addiction, and frequent communication with a schoolmate to build this narrative. Her schoolmates held a candlelight vigil to protest the defamation.

Renuka Chowdhury, then Minister for Women and Child Development, called for Inspector-General Singh's suspension. Singh was transferred a month later, only to be reinstated two months after.

Rajesh Talwar, claiming to be framed by the police to deflect attention from their mishandled investigation, saw the case transferred to the Central Bureau of Investigation (CBI) on May 31 at the request of Aarushi's parents. Under Joint-Director Arun Kumar IPS, the CBI commenced its probe in June.

In their defense, the Talwars presented several counter-arguments to the suspicions cast upon them. They contended that they slept through the murders due to the noise from two air conditioners in their rooms, a theory later supported by a sound expert team's recreation. They also challenged the initial theory of the murder scene, noting Hemraj's killing on the terrace and pointing out that Rajesh's clothes, as described by his driver and maid, only had Aarushi's blood and not Hemraj's. This suggested he wasn't involved in any sudden violent act.

Regarding the post-murder actions, the Talwars refuted claims of hastily cleaning the crime scene or dressing it up. They emphasized that if they had intended to do so, they wouldn't have left a bloodstained Scotch whisky bottle visible. They also maintained that the police had given permission to clean the house after collecting all necessary evidence.

Concerning access to Aarushi's room, Nupur suggested that the killer might have entered without force, possibly because she left the key in the door lock. Additionally, the Talwars and Durranis denied any allegations of an extramarital affair between Rajesh and Anita Durrani.

The Talwars further highlighted that neither of their fingerprints were found on key pieces of evidence, including the whisky bottle or the victims' clothes. Rajesh explained his focus on Hemraj as the prime suspect due to his disappearance and also expressed his lack of recollection regarding the police asking for the keys to the terrace door. He recounted his inability to recognize Hemraj's decomposed body, requiring confirmation from his wife, Nupur.

Due to the compromised crime scene, the CBI conducted polygraph, brain-mapping, and narco-analysis tests, all of which Rajesh and Nupur passed, indicating no evidence of deception.

Friends and relatives described observing the Talwars' profound grief, with Nupur's father noting Rajesh's hysterical state and a family friend speaking of Nupur's shock. Furthermore, a discrepancy was noted in the shoeprint size found on the terrace, which did not match Rajesh's shoe size, raising further questions about the police's initial theory.

In a gripping turn of events surrounding the case, the Talwars' version casts a shadow of doubt over Krishna Thadarai, an assistant in their dental clinic. They suggest that Thadarai, possibly aggrieved by a reprimand from Rajesh Talwar for a dental error, may have been involved in planting scandalous theories about Aarushi and Hemraj's relationship and Rajesh's alleged affair. Anita Durrani corroborated Rajesh's account of the reprimand, while Rajesh's driver, Umesh Sharma, recounted overhearing a heated conversation between Thadarai and Hemraj.

The intrigue deepened on 7 June, when the CBI detained Thadarai. A search of his home yielded a pillow cover, a blood-stained kukri (a traditional Nepalese knife), and trousers. Thadarai underwent multiple polygraph tests and a psychological assessment, followed by a Narco Analysis test, leading to his arrest on 13 June. Concurrently, lie detection tests on the Talwars remained inconclusive, with no evidence of deception in subsequent tests.

In a stunning revelation during his Narco test, Thadarai hinted at the involvement of a second perpetrator. This led the CBI to scrutinize his friend Rajkumar, a domestic worker with the Durranis. The investigation of Rajkumar included a series of forensic tests and the discovery of T-shirts with faint bloodstains at his residence. The Durranis suggested these could be from Rajkumar's boils. Rajkumar was arrested on suspicion on 27 June.

The case took another twist on 30 June 2008, with Vijay Mandal, a friend of Thadarai and an employee of the Talwars' neighbors, emerging as a suspect. Following a second Narco test on Rajkumar, media reports claimed he confessed to the murders, leading to further arrests, including Mandal's on 11 July.

In a later development, the Talwars filed a petition citing the Narco tests, which revealed the three suspects had watched a Nepali song on TV in Hemraj's room on the murder night. Nalini Singh, a journalist and owner of the Nepalese channel, confirmed that the song details matched the suspects' revelations, as informed by CBI official Anuj Arya.

At a critical press conference on July 11, 2008, Arun Kumar, a key figure in the investigation, announced that the perplexing Aarushi-Hemraj murder case remained unresolved. He clarified that while Rajesh Talwar was not found guilty, the CBI stopped short of completely absolving him. Kumar pointed to Thadarai, Rajkumar, and Mandal as likely suspects, based on their narco test results, yet he acknowledged the absence of solid corroborative evidence against them.

The narco tests themselves painted a confusing picture, with each of the three men presenting varying accounts of the events, and even individual inconsistencies within a single person's testimony. For instance, Thadarai's statements about the murder weapon changed three times.

Later that day, Rajesh Talwar was freed from his 50-day imprisonment due to insufficient evidence. He and Nupur moved to his parents' house following his release. Although the three suspects were detained, their drug-induced confessions were deemed insufficient for formal charges.

In a statement on August 9, 2008, CBI Director Ashwani Kumar reiterated the case's unsolved status but suggested that Rajesh Talwar should be cleared of suspicion. The three suspects were eventually released in September, as the police failed to gather concrete evidence against them.

Upon his release, Vijay Mandal accused the CBI of employing physical coercion and psychological tactics to force a confession or turn him into an informant against Thadarai and Rajkumar. He vehemently denied the charges, claiming innocence and asserting he had no prior acquaintance with Rajkumar. Mandal alleged that the CBI manipulated his semi-conscious state to extract false admissions.

In January 2009, the CBI was on the brink of filing charges against Thadarai, Rajkumar, and Mandal in the Aarushi-Hemraj case, but the lack of substantial evidence stalled this move.

A major controversy erupted in September 2009 when reports surfaced about the tampering of Aarushi Talwar's vaginal swab sample. The sample, collected by Dr. Sunil Dohre during the autopsy and sent to the Gautam Budh Nagar district hospital, became the center of a complex dispute. The hospital's record of Aarushi's sample mysteriously disappeared in 2008. Pathologist Dr. Ritcha Saxena, responsible for preparing the slides from the swabs, stated that the sample was handled by her technicians, Vikas and Navneet.

Dr. Saxena confirmed the absence of semen in the sample, which was then stored in a steel almirah in the hospital lab. On June 1, 2008, the CBI, seeking the sample, was guided by Dr. Saxena, then in Patna, to her lab. She claimed the sample was handed over to the CBI by Chief Medical Superintendent S C Singhal during her absence. Dr. Saxena and Singhal had a history of professional disputes, which she suggested might have influenced the handling of her records and the sample.

The CBI's CFSL lab in Delhi, led by Dr. BK Mohapatra, found the sample to be a mix of two different samples, including Aarushi's. Further testing by the CDFD in Hyderabad revealed predominant DNA from an unknown individual, leading to suspicions of a possible cover-up regarding evidence of sexual assault or consensual intercourse before Aarushi's death.

Dr. Saxena, acquainted with Aarushi's mother, Nupur Talwar, faced suspicion of tampering with the evidence. However, she vehemently denied any influence from Nupur Talwar and clarified her acquaintance with the Talwar family was minimal. The CBI's investigation into the Talwars and Dr. Saxena, including lie-detector and brain-mapping tests, and the examination of over a dozen vaginal swab slides, did not find conclusive evidence of tampering. Ultimately, the CBI attributed the mix-up to contamination, dismissing it as a mistake rather than a deliberate act of deception. Separately, Dr. Saxena faced dismissal due to absenteeism, unrelated to the case's controversies.

In July 2008 the Uttar Pradesh government decided to recall Arun Kumar, a 1985 batch IPS officer, to the UP cadre. The government clarified that this decision was not related to the Aarushi case. By September 2009, Kumar's tenure with the CBI concluded amid media allegations that he had neglected to investigate the suspected tampering scandal, leading to speculation about his removal from the case.

September 2009 saw the case handed over to a new CBI team led by SP Neelabh Kishore, with Additional SP AGL Kaul as the investigating officer. This team not only revisited previous suspicions against the parents but also brought forth new findings. They interrogated the doctors who performed Aarushi's autopsy, leading to Dr. Sunil Dohre's statement about the condition of Aarushi's hymen and cleaned private parts, and Dr. Naresh Raj's observation of Hemraj's physical state suggesting sexual activity. A crime scene analysis based on photographs also suggested that the scene had been altered post-murder.

A controversy arose when Dr. Dohre claimed that Dinesh Talwar, Aarushi's uncle, had asked him to speak to "Dr. Dogra" before the autopsy. Dohre thought he was speaking with AIIMS Forensics head Dr. TD Dogra, but this was later disproved. The CBI suspected Dinesh of trying to influence the autopsy report, a claim the defense argued was baseless.

The new CBI team identified a golf club as the likely weapon for the initial blow, suspecting one of Rajesh Talwar's clubs. Rajesh, an amateur golfer, had received a golf set from his neighbor years earlier. When the CBI requested this set in October 2009, Rajesh complied. Two clubs appeared conspicuously clean compared to the others, leading to suspicions they were cleaned to remove evidence. Rajesh maintained that these clubs had always been visible to investigators and had been moved to Hemraj's room by his driver before the murders.

Furthermore, Rajesh mentioned finding a golf club in his loft a year after the murders, but did not inform the CBI immediately. The defense highlighted that this was irrelevant since the golf set included two clubs numbered 5, one of which was the suspected murder weapon.

In May 2010, the Talwars were questioned by Nilabh Kishore in Dehradun. Subsequently, a report in The Pioneer suggested an honor killing angle, citing unnamed CBI sources. Rajesh Talwar filed for a restraint order against the misleading media reports in July. In response to a court notice, Kishore affirmed in October 2010 that no authorized CBI person had spoken to The Pioneer, dismissing the article as factually incorrect and speculative.

AGL Kaul, an officer with the CBI, later disclosed his inclination to file a chargesheet against Aarushi's parents for the murders. However, his superiors, Nilabh Kishore and Javed Ahmed, opted for a closure report citing a lack of sufficient evidence. Before finalizing this report, Arun Kumar from the first CBI team was consulted and he affirmed the absence of conclusive evidence linking the Talwars to the murder. This decision drew criticism from the Talwars' family and supporters, who accused the CBI investigators of being in collusion with the state police officers responsible for the initial botched investigation.

The closure report still named Rajesh Talwar as a suspect, prompting strong condemnation from the Talwars. Nupur Talwar expressed despair over the CBI's "false and baseless" allegations, feeling that their reputation was irreparably damaged. On January 24, 2011, this high-profile case took a violent turn when Rajesh Talwar was attacked by Utsav Sharma, a 29-year-old who claimed to be frustrated by the slow progress of the case. Sharma, previously known for assaulting S.P.S. Rathore in the Ruchika Girhotra Case, inflicted serious injuries on Rajesh with a meat cleaver. In the wake of the attack, Nupur criticized the CBI for indirectly inciting public hostility towards their family and lamented the sensationalist media coverage.

On January 30, 2011, a public demonstration demanding justice for Aarushi was held at Jantar Mantar. The protest saw participation from various activists, including members of the Middle Finger Protests group. They displayed banners with slogans like "CBI - Congress Bureau of Injustice" and "CBI - Congress Bureau of Investigation", reflecting widespread discontent with the investigative agency's handling of the case.

In January 2011, the Talwars filed a petition against the CBI's decision to close the Aarushi-Hemraj murder case, but their plea was dismissed by Preeti Singh, a magistrate of the special CBI court in Ghaziabad. On February 9, 2011, the closure report was converted into a charge sheet against the Talwars. Despite their efforts to challenge this decision in the Allahabad High Court and the Supreme Court, both courts rejected their appeals.

The trial officially commenced on May 11, 2013. The CBI's case was represented by senior advocate Siddharth Luthra, while the Talwars were defended pro bono by a team including former solicitor-general Harish Salve, Mukul Rohatgi, and Rebecca Mammen John. The defense focused on challenging the exoneration of Thadarai, Rajkumar, and Mandal, countering the suspicions against the Talwars, and highlighting investigative lapses. Although the Talwars had access to witness statements and photographs, they were not granted access to the polygraph, narco-analysis, and brain-mapping reports of the other suspects. The Supreme Court later rejected their request for these reports, deeming them inadmissible as evidence and accusing the Talwars of employing delaying tactics.

During the trial, it was reported that CBI officer AGL Kaul had used an email ID named after Hemraj for official communications with the Talwars, a tactic criticized as a pressure measure. The Talwars also requested touch DNA tests on various pieces of evidence, including a palm print on the terrace, a Scotch whisky bottle, and a golf club suspected as the murder weapon. However, these requests were denied by the Supreme Court, which also refused any further investigation.

In August 2012, CFSL DNA scientist BK Mahapatra claimed to have found male DNA on Aarushi's pillow, suggesting Hemraj's presence in her room. This claim was later refuted by the CBI, stating the pillow was actually from Hemraj's room. The defense argued that this mix-up was a deliberate attempt by the CBI to implicate the Talwars.

Additionally, the CBI sought to disprove the Talwars' claim that they couldn't hear the murders due to the noise from their air conditioner. They alleged that a plywood partition, not a brick wall, separated the rooms, and that the Talwars had hired a painter to modify the crime scene. The defense countered these claims, stating that the rooms were separated by a brick wall with plywood lamination and that the apartment was painted as part of a general renovation, approved by the CBI, long after the murders.

On November 25, 2013, a special CBI court found Rajesh and Nupur Talwar guilty of the two murders. The judge, Shyam Lal, convicted them on charges of murder, destruction of evidence, hindering the investigation, and filing an incorrect FIR. The following day, the couple was sentenced to life imprisonment.

The Talwar family decried the verdict as a failure of justice, asserting that the CBI had not presented key evidence that could have proven Rajesh and Nupur's innocence. Journalist Avirook Sen claimed that the judge had prepared the verdict before the defense had concluded their arguments. In response to the verdict, the Talwars filed an appeal in the Allahabad High Court in January 2014.

The High Court overturned the conviction on October 12, 2017, acquitting the Talwars. The court stated that the evidence against them was insufficient for a conviction beyond reasonable doubt, and they deserved the benefit of the doubt rather than a conviction based on suspicion. The High Court criticized the CBI's hypothesis regarding Hemraj's murder as implausible and absurd. However, Hemraj's family, including his wife Khumkala and brother Ashok Bhushal, disagreed with the verdict, believing the Talwars were guilty.

The trial and its outcome were scrutinized in a book titled 'The Killing of Aarushi and the Murder of Justice', which critiqued the judgment and the quality of evidence. The book suggested that the Aarushi case reflected broader issues of injustice in the Indian criminal justice system.

On March 8, 2018, the CBI filed an appeal against the acquittal in the Supreme Court. The Supreme Court accepted the CBI's appeal on August 10, indicating a continuation of the legal proceedings in this complex and high-profile case.

Murders of Dyke and Karen Rhoads

Paris, nestled in the eastern reaches of Illinois within the boundaries of Edgar County, presents itself as a quaint farming town. Once heralded as "The Midwest's most kept secret," Paris exudes a serene, almost idyllic ambiance, a stark contrast to the bustling cities elsewhere. It's a place where life moves at a gentler pace, and the community bonds are strong and enduring. However, beneath this tranquil veneer, Paris harbors a history tinged with mystery and intrigue, challenging the assumption that a town of its modest size could not be the setting for dark and hidden tales.

This narrative of contrast and hidden depths took a poignant turn on March 22, 1986. It was a day marked by joy and celebration for Dyke and Karen Rhoads, who exchanged their vows in the Lake Ridge Christian Church, surrounded by friends and family. Dyke, at 27, was an employee at Chemlawn Corporation in Terre Haute, Indiana, while Karen, 25, contributed her skills at the Morgan Manufacturing Plant, a venture of Robert Morgan.

The newlyweds, brimming with hopes and dreams, settled into their two-story abode at 433 E. Court Street in Paris. Their home became a testament to their profound love and the bright future they envisioned together. They were a couple deeply in love, eagerly anticipating a long, shared journey through life's highs and lows.

Tragically, the life they had envisaged was cut short, shrouded in circumstances that would leave the community and beyond grappling with questions and seeking closure. Their story, a blend of love, hope, and an unforeseen twist of fate, adds a poignant chapter to the history of Paris, challenging the town's quiet reputation and revealing the complexities and unexpected events that can unfold even in the most unassuming places.

In the serene farming town of Paris, Illinois, a chilling incident unfolded that would forever alter the community's tranquil reputation. Terry Newman, a local resident, lived in the vicinity of the Rhoads' home, a couple known for their deep love and commitment to each other. In the early hours of July 6, 1986, Newman's peaceful slumber was abruptly shattered. Around 4:00 a.m., the sharp, unmistakable sound of breaking glass pierced the night, jolting him awake. As he peered out his window, a horrific sight unfolded before his eyes: the Rhoads' house was being devoured by rampant flames, its structure illuminated by the fierce, orange glow of the fire.

Driven by a sense of urgency and concern for his neighbors, Newman dashed outside towards the inferno that had once been the Rhoads' sanctuary. He made his way to the south side of the house, where he was met with a locked side door. Desperation mounting, he pounded furiously on the door, hoping to rouse Dyke and Karen from their sleep. When no response came, he raced around to the front of the house, only to find the front door equally unyielding. Newman's screams, filled with panic and fear, echoed through the night, a futile attempt to alert the couple to the grave danger they were in.

Meanwhile, a female neighbor, sensing the gravity of the situation, contacted the fire department at 4:39 a.m. The firefighters arrived promptly, ready to battle the blaze and rescue any occupants. Once they managed to gain access to the house, a grim discovery awaited them. In the second-floor master bedroom, amidst the chaos and destruction wrought by the fire, lay the naked bodies of Dyke and Karen Rhoads. The scene was harrowing – the floor was splattered with blood, painting a stark and somber picture of the tragedy that had unfolded.

The fire, which had originated near the back of the house, had mercifully spared the front and second story from extensive damage. However, the master bedroom, the very heart of the couple's shared life and dreams, bore the scars of the fire and a far more sinister crime.

Edgar County Coroner David Dick was tasked with the somber duty of performing the autopsies on Dyke and Karen. The results were heartbreaking and disturbing. Dyke had suffered 28 stab wounds, primarily from behind, suggesting he was likely asleep when the brutal attack commenced. Karen's body told a story of struggle and desperation; she had 26 stab wounds, with defensive injuries on her hands indicating a fierce but ultimately futile fight for her life.

Further investigation into the couple's physical state revealed that Dyke had a blood alcohol level of .03 percent and .065 percent in his urine. There were no traces of drugs in his system. Similarly, no drugs or alcohol were found in Karen's system.

Edgar County States Attorney Michael McFatridge initially suggested that the killings were random. However, emerging details and recounted incidents hinted at a more complex and possibly sinister backstory, casting doubts on the randomness of these brutal acts.

Karen, a diligent worker at Morgan Manufacturing Company, had shared a chilling incident with her sister and brother-in-law that painted a picture of underlying tensions and possible threats. One evening, while at work, she received a phone call from a male caller urgently requesting to speak with her boss, Morgan. Karen, believing Morgan had left, informed the caller of this, only to notice Morgan still in the parking lot when she glanced out the window. The caller, emphasizing the importance of the conversation, requested Karen to convey a message to Morgan, referring to himself as 'Chicago.'

Compelled by a sense of duty, Karen approached Morgan, who was near his car, and was startled to find him carrying what appeared to be a machine gun. A quick look into the open trunk of his car revealed more machine guns, leading to an unsettling exchange. Morgan, taken aback by Karen's presence, admonished her, indicating that she should not have witnessed this scene. This encounter left Karen deeply disturbed, prompting her to confide in her brother-in-law, James Tate, about her intentions to resign from her job. James later reported this conversation to the Paris Police Department immediately following the murders, but, perplexingly, this interview was never officially documented.

Adding another layer to this complex narrative was Karen's past relationship with Tim Busby. Although their romantic involvement had ended, Karen maintained a close bond with Tim's mother, Marilyn Busby. During a lunch at a country club in Danville, Karen confided in Marilyn about her ongoing troubles at work, particularly with an employee named Mark "Smoke" Burba. Karen expressed her increasing discomfort and the worsening situation with Burba, leading her to consider seeking employment elsewhere.

Burba, known as Morgan's right-hand man, emerged as a recurring figure in the early stages of the murder investigation. Despite his name being mentioned multiple times and the concerning revelations shared by Karen, investigators surprisingly never questioned him. This oversight, or perhaps deliberate omission, in the investigation added to the growing suspicions and unanswered questions surrounding the case. The failure to follow these leads left a shadow of doubt over the investigation, suggesting that the tragic fate of Dyke and Karen Rhoads might not have been a random act of violence but a calculated and targeted crime, intricately linked to the hidden undercurrents within the small town of Paris.

One particularly striking aspect of the case was the handling of key figures by the authorities, which was later brought to light by author and retired Illinois State Police investigator Michale Callahan in his book on the Paris murders.

Callahan highlighted the minimal scrutiny given to Robert Morgan, a significant figure in the community and Karen's employer. Despite the potential connections and the mysterious incident involving Karen at work, Morgan was only interviewed once by the police. Investigator Jack Eckerty, years later, shed light on this perplexing oversight. He revealed that Morgan was always considered a suspect, yet there was a deliberate shift in focus away from him and other potential suspects. This redirection, according to Eckerty, was influenced by Edgar County States Attorney Michael McFatridge, who seemed to have other targets in mind.

McFatridge's focus centered intensely on two individuals: Herb Whitlock and Gordon Randy Steidl. His determination to pin the crime on them was unwavering, regardless of the potential inconsistencies or questionable tactics required. The pursuit of these suspects took a significant turn on January 21, 1987. Herb Whitlock, then 41, found himself pleading guilty to the unlawful possession of a controlled substance. This charge stemmed from an arrest on April 5, 1986, where he was allegedly caught with 15.6 grams of cocaine by Edgar County Sheriff's deputies.

A mere month after Whitlock's guilty plea, a dramatic development occurred. Officers from the Paris Police Department and the Illinois State Police arrested Gordon Randy Steidl, a 35-year-old construction worker. Both Steidl and Whitlock were charged with the murder of Dyke and Karen Rhoads. Intriguingly, they were not charged with arson at the time, a detail that added to the growing complexity and confusion surrounding the case.

In March 1987, the case took another turn. A Grand Jury hearing was convened, during which McFatridge presented his theory. He claimed that Steidl and Whitlock were responsible for the murders of Dyke and Karen Rhoads, alleging the motive was a sour drug deal. This theory, and the subsequent focus on Steidl and Whitlock, diverted attention from other potential leads and suspects, weaving a narrative of selective investigation and questionable judicial process.

Edgar County States Attorney Michael McFatridge presented a narrative to the jury that painted a vivid and chilling picture of the events leading to the couple's tragic end. He posited that on July 6, 1986, two men, Steidl and Whitlock, had convened at a local bar with a plan to pursue a specific woman. McFatridge suggested that the evening's events spiraled into a sinister plot involving several individuals.

The prosecution's story hinged significantly on the testimony of 30-year-old Debra Reinbolt. According to McFatridge's account, Reinbolt, along with Steidl, Whitlock, and another individual named Derrell Herrington, left the bar and subsequently arrived at the Rhoads' home. In a harrowing description, McFatridge claimed that Reinbolt was complicit in the crime, alleging that she restrained Karen while Steidl and Whitlock used a knife, purportedly borrowed from Reinbolt, to fatally stab Dyke. Following this, Whitlock was said to have turned the weapon on Karen.

The narrative further detailed that Herrington, reportedly asleep in the car during the murders, was later taken into the house by Steidl to witness the aftermath. McFatridge portrayed a scene where Steidl, showing Herrington the bodies, issued a grave threat to ensure his silence. The culminating act of this alleged crime involved the two men setting fires in the kitchen and bedroom using gasoline.

However, the credibility of the witnesses central to McFatridge's case was highly questionable. Herrington, known in the town for his alcoholism and with a history of felony arrests and mental health issues, initially claimed to have knowledge of the murders stemming from a botched drug deal involving Dyke. His involvement in the crime scene and his allegations against Steidl and Whitlock raised doubts, especially considering Dyke's limited drug use history and the lack of any mention of Reinbolt's presence by Herrington.

Two years after his initial statement, Herrington recanted, alleging that he was under the influence of alcohol provided by the police during his interview.

He claimed that police officers had kept him intoxicated both at the station and at a private residence, deceiving his wife about his whereabouts.

Reinbolt, the other key witness, emerged with her statement five months after Herrington. Her own credibility was equally dubious. A self-admitted alcoholic and drug user, Reinbolt's lifestyle between 1985 and 1987 involved heavy consumption of beer, marijuana, amphetamines, and cocaine. This background severely undermined the reliability of her testimony.

The trial thus unfolded with two central witnesses whose accounts were fraught with inconsistencies and personal issues that cast a shadow over their reliability. The decision to rely on the testimonies of Herrington and Reinbolt, given their backgrounds and subsequent revelations, pointed to a deeply flawed approach in the pursuit of justice for the tragic deaths.

In May 1987, the murder trial of Herb Whitlock commenced, marking the beginning of a complex and controversial legal journey. Represented by defense attorney Ron Tulin, Whitlock faced the severe allegations stemming from the tragic deaths of Dyke and Karen Rhoads. Following closely, in June 1987, the trial of Gordon Randy Steidl began, with John Muller of Charleston serving as his defense attorney. These trials, set against the backdrop of a small Illinois town, would unfold into a drama rife with twists, turns, and deepening mysteries.

Central to both trials were the testimonies of Debra Reinbolt and Derrell Herrington, who provided detailed accounts of the events on July 6, 1986. Reinbolt's narrative was particularly graphic and distressing. She claimed that what began as an attempt to merely intimidate Dyke Rhoads spiraled out of control into a violent and fatal altercation. Reinbolt described witnessing both Whitlock and Steidl stabbing Dyke, while she herself was involved in a harrowing act of restraining Karen Rhoads during her attack.

Reinbolt's story was not just compelling in its detail; it also included specific elements that resonated with the police, such as her accurate description of a broken lamp found in the Rhoads' bedroom. This seemingly minute detail lent a degree of credibility to her account in the eyes of law enforcement.

Despite a lack of physical evidence linking Whitlock and Steidl to the crime scene, the weight of the eyewitness testimonies carried significant influence in the courtroom. Both juries, swayed by the graphic and detailed accounts of Reinbolt and Herrington, found the narratives presented by the prosecution convincing. In a stunning verdict that year, Whitlock and Steidl were convicted of the murders. Whitlock received a life sentence for the murder of Karen Rhoads, while Steidl was handed the death penalty for his role in both killings.

The convictions, however, were mired in controversy and doubt. There were unwavering protests of innocence from both Whitlock and Steidl, and other witnesses provided alibis, claiming the men were with them on the night of the murders. This lack of physical evidence and conflicting testimonies raised serious questions about the jury's decision-making process. Particularly perplexing was the discrepancy in the convictions – Steidl was found guilty of both murders, whereas Whitlock was only convicted for the murder of Karen. This inconsistency in the jury's verdicts added a layer of complexity and doubt to an already intricate and deeply troubling case, leaving many to ponder the intricacies of the justice system and the weight of eyewitness testimony in the balance of truth and justice.

In 1999, a significant breakthrough emerged in the long and tumultuous saga of Herb Whitlock and Gordon Randy Steidl, who had been convicted in the controversial murders of Dyke and Karen Rhoads. After years of enduring prison life and maintaining their innocence, help arrived in an unexpected form.

David Protess, a journalism professor at Northwestern University, known for his investigative prowess and his role in uncovering wrongful convictions, took an interest in the case. Along with four of his dedicated students, Protess embarked on a mission to delve deeper into the details of the crime, driven by a strong suspicion that a miscarriage of justice had occurred. This was not unfamiliar territory for Protess, as his previous investigations had played pivotal roles in proving the innocence of several individuals wrongfully convicted of murder.

Protess was immediately struck by the glaring absence of physical evidence connecting Steidl and Whitlock to the brutal crime scene. The sheer brutality of the murders, with the young couple stabbed over 50 times, led Protess to reason that the real perpetrators would have been significantly marked by the violence of their act. Blood, a tell-tale sign in such violent encounters, would have been present on the assailants' clothing, in their vehicles, and likely left behind in the form of other forensic evidence such as hair or fibers. Yet, remarkably, none of these traces were found to link Steidl and Whitlock to the scene, an anomaly that raised serious doubts about the integrity of the conviction.

This re-investigation, spearheaded by Protess and his team, eventually bore fruit. In 2004, after years of legal battles and growing scrutiny over the evidence, Steidl was released from prison. Four years later, in 2008, Whitlock also regained his freedom, marking the end of a harrowing journey for both men.

The aftermath of their release was not just a quiet return to normalcy. In 2013, Steidl achieved a significant legal victory, winning a second multi-million-dollar judgment in his case against those responsible for his wrongful conviction and incarceration. This followed a similar triumph in 2011 against the Illinois State Police. These victories not only offered financial compensation but also served as a public acknowledgment of the grievous errors that had led to their unjust imprisonment. The case of Steidl and Whitlock stands as a stark reminder of the fallibility of the criminal justice system and the profound impact investigative journalism can have in righting the wrongs of the past.